A FEW AC(

Hello Dale,

My name is Sean McGroarty. My wife Diane and I met you on the driving range at Terra Lago on Saturday morning. You gave Diane and me some impromptu golf instructions. You were so nice and we were so impressed with your willingness to help and the simple way in which you explained the technical aspects of our swings. We listened and went out and played the best round we have played in a while. Diane actually had her first ever Eagle on the 2nd hole of the north course, the number one handicap hole (picture attached). Wow. We were so excited I decided to Google you. I only knew your first name, but with clues from our conversation, I was able to locate you and subsequently purchased your book. Thanks so much for opening our eyes. We hope to see you again next time we are in Indio. Sean McGroarty

Dale, you presented the images about the golf swing in a very unique way that provided an excellent way of understanding the swing. Al Slavich, Vancouver, WA

When starting out at any new sport, the proper guidance is key to succeeding. Reading this book truly helped me perfect my game. Now, I'm winning tournaments and competing in USGA events. Jon McCaslin

INSTANT GOLF LESSONS
Make Sense Golf Instruction

by

Dale McNall

Summit Bay Press
Olympia WA

INSTANT GOLF LESSONS
Make Sense Golf Instruction

Copyright © 2000 by Dale McNall
Republished 2021

ISBN: 9798773228486

Printed in the United States of America

All rights reserved. No part of this work may be reproduced or used in any form or by any means—graphic, electronic, or mechanical, including photocopying or information storage or retrieval systems—without written permission from the author.

The scanning, uploading, and distribution of this book or any part thereof via the Internet or any other means without the permission of the author is illegal and punishable by law. Please purchase only authorized editions and do not participate in or encourage the electronic piracy of copyrighted materials.

DEDICATION

To all golfers of different ages and physical abilities:
This golf instruction will enhance your playing the great game of golf.

A NOTE FROM THE AUTHOR

The old gray-haired senior in the acknowledgements is me. My name is Dale McNall, the author of this book. Although I have been teaching golf for many years, telling you how great my teaching methods are and how great the results have been is not going to help you. Telling you how good some of the people I have helped can play golf, I am sure will not help you play better either.

What will help you play better is what you read and learn in this instruction book. These golf swing instructions are simplified fundamentals and swing philosophy for learning a powerful, smooth golf swing.

CREDENTIALS

Up to the writing of this book (as of 2000), I had spent over fifty years teaching golf. Originally, I taught at a driving range, later a golf course, and then quit to spend more time with my family. Later on, due to a request from my son, I taught his high school class along with teaching their golf coach and his son. I took one of the students to California to play the tour qualifying Bayonet Course in Monterey, the Rio Bravo Course in Bakersfield, and Chardonnay Course in Napa. My best young student played his way onto the Canadian Tour by winning a Monday qualifying spot: there were 134 participants for two spots. He went on to get two third-place finishes out of three events played. I wrote a couple of golf books: one right hand, one left hand. I stopped self-publishing the left hand and continued to self-publish the right-hand instruction book—this one. It was too confusing for left-handed golfers to read the instructions straight out, for they are so used to turning instructions around in their heads. I have continued to give lessons, teach and help all golfers anywhere I am.

THIS BOOK IS FOR YOU

If you would like an easy way to learn how to accomplish a smooth, natural, flowing golf swing and follow-through, to hit the ball more accurately and farther, then this book is for you. If you would like to put your flexibility back into your golf swing, then this book is for you. If you would like a quick way to get rid of existing poor swing habits, then this book is for you. If you would like to take the stress off your sore joints, then this book is for you. If you would like to put some consistency into your golf swing, then this book is for you. If you would like to learn to put your shoulders on swing planes to hit draw and fade shots, then this book is for you. If you have aspirations of teaching the golf swing to someone else, then this book is for you.

I can say as a golf teacher, it has always been in my heart to help as many people as possible to learn the golf swing anywhere and any place. This book is my way of very quickly helping you and a lot more golfers learn and maintain a good golf swing. This book gives me the ability to help a lot more people than ever possible in person.

In closing, I would like to say that so many people I have helped have said to me: One, they wish they would have started playing golf at a younger age. Two, they wish they had started with this book.

ACKNOWLEDGEMENTS

I would like to thank all my friends who have helped me put this teaching instrument together.

I would especially like to thank the young lad on the left in this photo, Scott Geroux, Professional Golfer. Scott let me put him in all the swing positions while I took pictures. I have been Scott's swing teacher for twenty-three years. I treat him like one of the family—a real nice lad. I tell you, Scott can really play golf: He was a three time All American at Weber State, Ogden, Utah; placed third in two of the three Canadian Tour events entered, and took the lead in the last round at one of the events before dropping back to third. Scott is now playing on the Cascade Tour in Washington State. Since this book was written in 1999-2000, he has won five ties, placed second twice, and has had eight top ten finishes. Of course, his real goal is to play on the PGA Tour of America.

2021 Update: Since writing the original book, Scott developed a crippling finger and hand disorder, which ended his quest to play on the professional tour.

A special thank you to my significant other, Rose Green, and Joel Graves—Lacey, WA, my golfing buddy, for help in editing and reformatting this book for regular publication.

TABLE OF CONTENTS

DEDICATION iv
ACKNOWLEDGEMENTS vii
INTRODUCTION xiii
CHAPTER ONE *Lower Body* 1
    LIFTING THE HEELS 6
    KNEES 8
    HOW THE LEFT HEEL RELATES TO THE BACKSWING 9
    WHAT GETS YOUR GOLF BACKSWING INTO TROUBLE 11
    HOW TO GET YOUR GOLF BACKSWING
    OUT OF TROUBLE 11
    INITIATING YOUR BACKSWING AND FORWARD SWING
    CORRECTLY 13
    INITIATING YOUR FORWARD SWING CORRECTLY 14
    HOW THE REVERSE WEIGHT SHIFT RELATES TO THE
    FORWARD SWING 17
    KEY TO A SMOOTH SWING 18
    KEEP YOUR HEAD STEADY, NOT DOWN 19
    THE MAJOR DIFFERENCE BETWEEN THE LEFT
    KNEE AND RIGHT KNEE 21
    THE LOWER BODY EXECUTES THE START OF THE
    FORWARD SWING 23
    WHY YOU WANT TO KEEP SWINGING BACK AND FORTH
    WITHOUT STOPPING 25

THE PROPER WIDTH IN THE STANCE AND DISTANCE
FROM THE BALL 27

KEEP YOUR HEAD AND SHOULDERS UP EVEN IF YOU
WEAR GLASSES 34

CHAPTER TWO *How to Grip the Club* 39

PLACING THE CLUB UNDER THE HEEL OF THE LEFT HAND
FOR BETTER GRIP 39

PLACING THE RIGHT HAND BEHIND THE SHAFT 45

CHAPTER THREE *Ball Position, Stance and Set Up* 49

THE STANCE AND ADDRESS POSITION 50

SET UP ROUTINE 53

NEVER PLACE YOUR LEFT FOOT FIRST 54

CHAPTER FOUR *Upper Body* 57

CONSTANT SHOULDER PLANE 57

CHECK YOUR SHOULDER PLANE 59

NATURAL AIMING METHOD FOR THE
SHOULDER PLANE 61

HOW FAST DO YOU SWING THE GOLF CLUB IN YOUR
BACKSWING? 65

THE RIGHT ELBOW WORKS AS A LEVER IN
THE FORWARD SWING 67

THE RIGHT ARM MOVEMENT IS LIKE SKIPPING ROCKS 68

GOLF IS A TWO-HANDED GAME 70

THE PROPER ADDRESS POSITION AND
SWING MOTIONS 73

SWING MOMENTUM AND TOTAL EXTENSION OF THE
ARMS PULLS THE HEAD UP 77
THE TAKEAWAY OR START OF THE BACKSWING 79
SWINGING IN A CIRCLE 80
HANGING ON TOO LONG WITH THE LEFT HAND 83
COMING OVER THE TOP AND TOO MUCH
RIGHT HAND 84
TOO MUCH HOOK 86
TOO MUCH SLICE 86

CHAPTER FIVE *Equipment* 89

CHAPTER SIX *Practice and Playing Procedures* 93
THE SUBCONSCIOUS AND THE SHORT GAME 95
BEING IN THE ZONE 99
NERVES, PRESSURE AND FEAR 100
SOME PLAYING PROCEDURES AND GOLF ETIQUETTE 101
READY GOLF 104

PARTING SHOTS 109
CONTACT INFORMATION 109
GLOSSARY 110
AFTERWORD 114

INTRODUCTION

I always said that when I wrote my first golf book this would be the first statement:

Improving your body posture, along with enhancing your body mechanics, can and will improve your golf swing.

What makes golf so difficult?

We play many games in life while growing up: baseball, football, darts, and bowling are just a few. All of the aforementioned games are played looking at your target while your eyes, along with your brain, control what to do with the object you are throwing or rolling.

If you were playing football and you are the quarterback, you can see the target or player you are throwing to, you can see the defensive player, you can judge visionally their speed and distance from you to them, and throw the football with your throwing arm. Your eyes help you constantly in all phases of throwing the football or any object at a target.

Now in golf, we do not have the help from our eyes, we are looking down at a singular object—the golf ball—while executing the golf swing. We are not looking at the target as in football. We have our eyesight, swing memory, or subconscious concentration all on the ball, while making the golf swing. In comparison, this would be like trying to throw the football while having all our concentration on the ball, not looking to where we were going to throw the football.

Otherwise, try throwing the football to your player while staring at the ball and not looking where to throw it. This singular thing is what makes golf so difficult: you have no input from your eyes to help execute all the moving body parts in the physical golf swing. We have only a picture in our minds (subconscious) of what the swing feels and looks like.

For you to make any changes to your golf swing, even minor changes, it affects your subconscious, and the subconscious relearns any changes slowly. So be patient.

This is why they say, golf is ninety percent mental. It is not because we are trying to solve difficult quadratic equations. No, we execute the golf swing mechanics, grip, stance, posture, including feel, all through our subconscious.

This is where I want to again emphasize how important it is that you understand that unlearning pre-existing swing thoughts you have in your subconscious is not easy but not impossible. So be patient with yourself.

I have been on the practice tee with a student, showing them a change to make in their golf grip. They make several swings with the new grip or hit several balls, then they are right back to the old grip without thinking, because that is what the subconscious is comfortable with. Even though with a little practice the new grip would enhance the ability to play golf immensely better. It is very gratifying when a student says, the new grip has increased my swing yardage and ball striking consistency.

Once you read this book, come back to the list below. Experience the after effect of seeing how easy it is, not only to tell which items in the list are swing misconceptions, but what causes common swing faults, body pain, and how you can correct them.

Have you ever heard these comments?

- You looked up
- You rose up during the swing
- You tried to kill it
- You hit behind the ball
- You have a reverse pivot
- You swing from the top
- You pulled the ball to the left
- You straightened your right leg on the backswing
- You sliced
- You hooked
- You topped the ball
- You hit the ball with too much right hand
- You hit the ball but hang on too long with the left hand
- I'm older and not as flexible
- My back hurts
- My knee hurts

You can eliminate all these and other problems by learning and understanding how the body works in the golf swing!

My intention in writing this book is to teach you to strike the golf ball using the natural movements and functions of your body during the golf swing. You will learn how your natural body movements affect the golf swing, both good and bad. This understanding will greatly enhance your ability to improve your golf swing. You will be able to make changes in your swing to coincide with your natural body movements. You will also avoid years of frustration and improve your swing mechanics immediately.

Over the years, I have helped many people, from beginners to professionals, immediately improve their swing mechanics. I can cite many instances where this statement has become a reality. Often, I've taken a few minutes to teach someone on the driving range. After giving a little instruction on the shoulder swing plane, someone who has been constantly fading or slicing the golf ball to the right started drawing the ball immediately to the left.

Or, I'd teach someone the proper leg movements which allowed him or her to follow-through and finish their swing correctly for the first time ever—with a look of sheer delight!

I was able to help these people in a matter of minutes. Some of them were beginners and others had been golfing for over forty years. Some were kids and others were in their nineties. Many were golfers who had already acquired and locked in bad swing habits. They were all able to make immediate improvements. These joyous occasions have been very rewarding to me, as well as to the golfers I have helped. I want to help you, too!

As the student, you must have a sincerity and commitment to achieve this goal. Having already played golf, you can quickly eliminate bad habits and mold yourself into a better golfer. The student and the teacher must bond and trust each other.

I have one goal: To teach you to become a smooth swinging golfer.

When it comes to golfers making changes in their golf swing, some golfers dive right into any change with the objective to be a better golfer. Others are more cautious and have said, while making the slightest change, "That doesn't feel right." It's very important for you to remember that I understand; it does take time and practice to become comfortable with changes you make, even little ones, while acquiring new swing habits. I will give you some drills along the way to make you comfortable in achieving these new swing tasks more quickly. If you're ready, let's get started immediately.

It may be advantageous to read the whole book then come back to the beginning and go over each instruction thoroughly.

All explanations in the book are for a right-handed golfer and just the opposite for a left-handed golfer.

CHAPTER ONE
Lower Body

When someone tells you that you looked up, or lifted up, or tried to kill the ball, what do you think caused these problems? Do you think that while you are swinging, you are so anxious to see where the ball is going that you look up before hitting the ball? Or, do you think the problem is that you take one last look at your target and then swing too fast and too hard? Do you think to yourself that the causes and cures for these problems are the upper body or everything from the waist up? Of course, you would. That's where the arms and head are.

So, you've tried correcting these problems by keeping your head down (Figure 1), not swinging too hard with your arms, and keeping yourself from rising up. Believe it or not, your conclusions are erroneous. These remedies are temporary at best, and in most cases, only make things worse.

The cure for these problems is from the waist down.

The initial weight on your right leg at the start of your backswing, and the additional weight loaded onto the right leg as you're swinging your golf club back, are perfect for completion of the backswing.

The problem occurs (Figure 1) when you start the forward/down swing with a body movement called a Reverse Weight Shift. Look closely at the forward swing and follow-through in Figure 1. The reverse weight shift starts at the beginning of your forward swing.

- Too much weight has remained on your left leg during the backswing.
- The weight from your left leg is transferred to the right or thrust onto your right leg from the momentum of your forward swing.
- This excess weight forces the right heel to remain on the ground throughout the forward swing and follow-through.

Fig. 1

This incorrect position causes numerous problems. One problem is that it forces your head up and out of the golf shot. If you are in the correct swing posture at impact, *you cannot lift your head*. At the point of impact, where the club meets the ball, the muscles in your left shoulder are in a neutral position and almost feel like they are being compressed.

Look at the correct swing impact position in Figure 2, and then try it yourself. Place the club head behind the ball, as if in a stationary hitting position. Lift your right heel and point your knee just in front of the ball. Let your left hip and side rotate to the left without moving your left shoulder. If you are into the golf shot correctly, and in the ball striking area on the forward swing, it will be the same as standing in this stationary position. The inside of your left shoulder will be close to the lower left side of your face. Your left shoulder will be pointing just right of the target. Your muscles do not have enough strength in a neutral position to lift your head.

As in Figure 2, the muscles between your neck and shoulder should be neutral. Try it in a different way without a golf club and from a normal standing position. Push your left shoulder as close as you can to your cheek, and then try to lift your head. You can feel that it is very difficult to raise your head in this position, disproving the notion that you looked up too soon, unless you are born with a special look up muscle, then I can't help you.

Muscles in a neutral position are like rubber bands, just lying on a table. Nothing happens until you pull on the rubber band, which puts it in tension. If the muscles are in tension, that's a different story. If during the forward swing you have weight on your right leg, it becomes rigid trying to support the body. This causes a reverse shift in your hips, pulls on the back muscles, and forces your left shoulder to fly to the left.

Your shoulder muscles are thrown into tension because your body is forced to take the line of least resistance. Thus, like a rope towing a car, your head will be towed out of position. Your fellow golfer might erroneously say that *you looked up.* You can see the incorrect swing position in Figure 3. These drastic chain reactions occur:

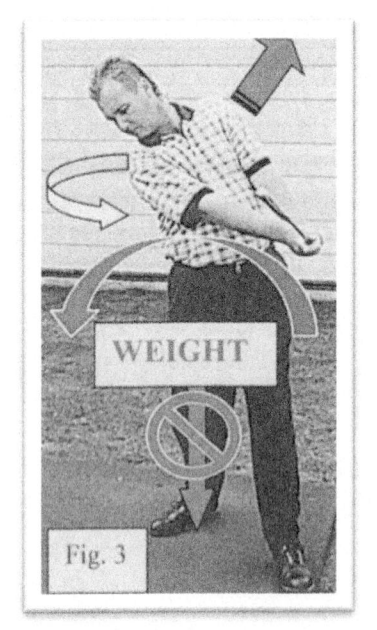

- Falling back with the little extra weight added to your right knee, which causes your lower right leg to be rigid.
- It's the rigidity in your right leg that pulls on the back muscles, causing your left shoulder muscles to be in tension.
- Your head is pulled out of position from the tension in the upper left shoulder muscles—between neck and left shoulder.

This chain of events forces your hands quickly left, along with the club head, resulting in a miss-hit golf shot. The causes of these problems are occurring from your waist down. The remaining weight, plus the additional weight transferred to your right leg during the forward swing, is forcing all unwanted upper body movement.

4

Your body will not go where there is resistance. It will always take the line of least resistance. If the weight remains on the right leg during the forward swing, it spins the upper body sharply to the left. That causes a resistance or blocking in the upper torso, which will not allow the arms and hands to follow-through or release toward the target. Instead, the club head, along with the upper torso, will turn sharply left during and after contact with the ball. Your body is following the line of least resistance.

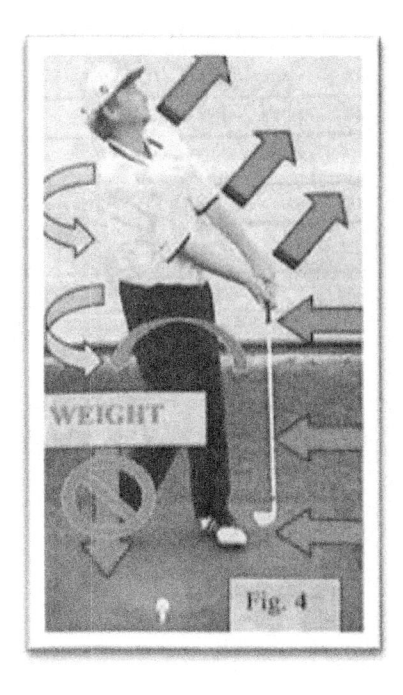

In Figure 4, you can see this awkward incorrect forward swing position.

<< Reverse weight shift on right leg causes a blocking or resistance to the swing at the target, because the left shoulder, arm and hands are forced sharply left, following the line of least resistance and tension.

Again, the correction to most of these problems is in the lower body from the waist down. For most golfers, the back leg—or in this case the right leg—is the cause of most problems more than anything else, excluding the grip. It is what causes pains in your knees, hip joints and back.

Thus, my focus is to teach you the lower body swing movements first. This is a real key to helping you develop a

5

natural, fluid swing, removing any of the resistance/tension in your golf swing.

Your natural walking motion is in each golf swing.

First, let's concentrate on our natural leg movements. Our legs shift the weight from one side to the other, as illustrated in Figures 5 and 6. When we walk down the street, we don't have to think right side, left side. This happens naturally. The moment our heel clears the ground, our body weight is shifted onto the other leg. These are the very same motions we should use in the golf swing to eliminate tension.

LIFTING THE HEELS

Let's see how the natural leg and foot action while walking relates to the proper leg action in the golf swing.
Try this: Stand up straight without a golf club, your feet about six inches apart, weight evenly distributed. Next, lift your left heel about one-half inch off the floor. You will find that as the left heel raises and your left knee bends, you are standing with the weight shifted onto your right leg.

So, lifting your left heel starts the back swing.

Figure 5 Left heel up so weight transfers to right foot in the golf backswing.
Now, let's start over and try the right leg. Lift your right heel and bend your right knee. You are standing with the weight shifted onto your left leg.

So, right heel lift starts the forward swing.

Also, notice that the knee joint bends only when the heel has cleared the ground and there is no weight on that leg.

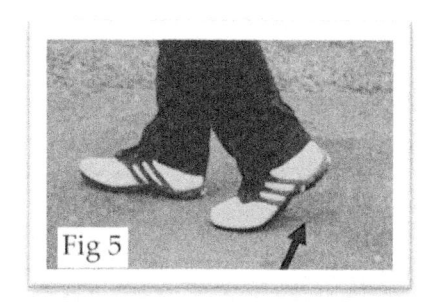

Fig 5

Figure 6 Right heel up, so weight shifts to your left foot as you swing forward.

The inability to lift your heels in the golf swing is what I call poor foot and leg action. Because of the weight on your leg, you are unable to lift the heel of that foot. This restricts the ability to properly shift your weight from one leg to the other during the swing.

Fig 6

While you are walking, relate it to the golf swing. Think about each step you take. While walking, the leg you put your weight on stays rigid to support your body. At the start of the forward swing, if your right leg has the slightest additional weight thrust onto it--let's say just the additional weight of a copper penny—your right leg will stay rigid! This is called a reverse weight shift. Your right knee will lock in to support your body, just as it does while you're walking.

NOTE: Lifting your heels is a natural movement of the feet and legs while walking as well as in swinging the golf club. Your body is used to raising the heels; your golf subconscious is not. It will take some time and patience to change lifting your heels to your golf swing.

KNEES

Knees, in general, can do very little bending with the full body weight on the legs. Pictures in golf magazines often give you the impression that the knees are moving sideways in the lower part of the golf swing. *The creator gave us knees that move forward and back to their original position, not sideways!* You are only able to obtain some lateral movement in your knees because of our hip and ankle joints.

TEST THIS FOR YOURSELF

While standing, put about seventy percent of your weight on your right leg. Try moving your right knee sideways, left or right. Your knee can't go sideways. When seventy percent of the weight is on the right leg only, a slight motion left or right can occur, and that's from your ankle and hip joints. Now squat down a little to make your right knee go forward and then back to its original position. At this point, it's even hard to make your right knee go forward.

Knees only work well with the weight off the leg. A knee does not function well with the weight on the leg. If you have poor leg action due to your weight not shifting properly, you will have sore joints at the end of your golf game.

I am trying to teach you that the proper leg action will not only improve your golf game, but it will eliminate a lot of back and joint pain too. Nothing adds more pain to your back, hips, and knees than swinging with the weight on the right foot and leg while swinging forward.

Remember, in your golf swing, your knees work for you when you're able to shift your weight properly from one leg to the other.

HOW THE LEFT HEEL RELATES TO THE BACKSWING

If you **_do not_** lift your left heel at the beginning of the backswing, many natural things happen:

1. You force your right leg to straighten at the knee from its original flexed position.

2. The right knee movement reduces your left shoulder turn and pushes your weight back to your left leg.

3. Your weight has transferred to your left side or the wrong side.

4. This movement puts pressure on your back and left knee during the backswing.

5. At the start or the initial thrust of your forward swing your weight is transferred back to your right leg with your weight being transferred again to the wrong side.

So, you have a reverse weight shift. This reverse weight shift will put pressure on your back, knees and especially your right knee during your forward swing. It is **_not natural_** for your body to leave your left heel anchored to the ground while walking or during your full swing of the golf shot.

TEST THIS THEORY

Try walking naturally, without raising your left heel. Obviously, you can tell that keeping your left heel down while walking is not a natural body movement. You wouldn't lift your right heel, take a step with your right foot, and then slide your left foot along the ground without lifting your left heel to move your left foot forward.

You should use the same natural foot movements in your golf swing as you use while walking.

One important thing I observe in almost all golfers that leave their left heel anchored to the ground is their left shoulder rotation is restricted. The right leg is forced to straighten slightly at the knee. This causes a down force on the left leg at the top of the backswing, putting a strain or restriction of movement on the left knee action. The left shoulder is then forced to quit turning because of the restriction. The arms move out of the natural swing plane because the left shoulder is forced down below the swing plane.

Learn to use the correct weight transfer in your golf swing. The following will address how you get into trouble and how to get out of a reverse weight shift.

WHAT GETS YOUR GOLF BACKSWING INTO TROUBLE

If during the start of the backswing, the heel of your left foot is anchored to the ground, not lifting your left heel slightly causes your weight to slightly lean forward to the left side or remain on your forward leg at the top of your back swing. Then when you start to thrust the swing forward, additional weight from the leaning to the left will move towards your back foot making it impossible to get off your back foot on the forward swing. The weight will remain on your back foot or right leg throughout the forward swing. This movement of a reverse weight shift is disastrous to the golf swing in many ways. The reverse weight forces your head up, makes you feel like you swung too fast, tried to kill it, and forces you to step out of the golf shot. Of course, you will hear this: you looked up and tried to kill it.

HOW TO GET YOUR GOLF BACKSWING OUT OF TROUBLE

Again, weight should go from your forward foot to your back foot on the backswing, and from your back foot to your forward foot on the forward swing. Swinging in a circle. By lifting your heels, you will be able to do this. Address the ball with your knees bent slightly. On the back swing, raising your left heel simultaneously with taking the club back, keeping the right knee bent, turning your body in a circle like being in a barrel. You will feel the tension has been removed from your golf back swing. Raise your right heel as you start the forward swing, and you will finish the forward swing facing the target, all your weight on your left leg and balanced by the toe of your right foot.

Your new golf swing will remove all the aforementioned swing faults, while removing the pain in your joints as you turn onto your left or forward leg in comfort and not with all the weight being on the back leg as your body is trying to turn in a circle left, twisting your knee joint and hurting your back.

The reverse weight transfer forces your forward swing to start from the waist up—from the upper body. This in turn causes numerous problems, such as swinging with the arms only, which results in loss of power and distance. Moreover, the poor leg action is what causes many golfers to suffer lower back pain and sore knees. Some famous professional golfers, who have habitually left their left heel flat on the ground while swinging, are now suffering serious back problems.

Constant restriction in a natural leg movement will aggravate the lower spine and back muscles.

TEST IT FOR YOURSELF

As in Figure 7, leave your left heel flat on the ground and take a backswing. You can feel your left shoulder turn under stress and restriction as your arms reach just above waist high.

Now start over, and this time raise your left heel about one-half inch, rotate your hips to the right, and point your left knee just behind the ball. You can feel that the left shoulder restriction is reduced, and your weight transfer is completed to your right leg immediately upon lifting your left heel. It's the same motion as when you are walking. The result is you have better leg action and a longer backswing with your shoulders turning further.

People who are not as flexible may raise their heel higher than one-half inch, as long as they point the left knee just behind the ball and return their heel to its original position during the forward swing.

Fig. 7

Right knee is forced to straighten

WEIGHT

INITIATING YOUR BACKSWING AND FORWARD SWING CORRECTLY

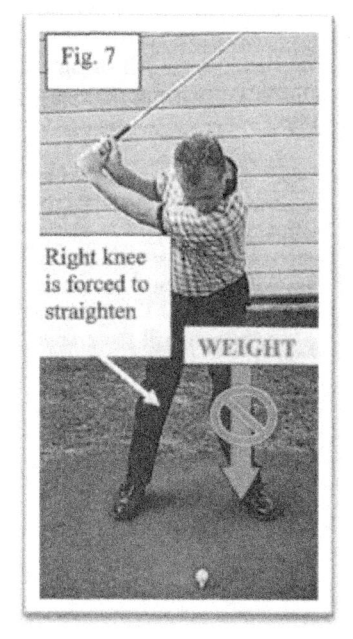

Let's review the correct leg movements, initiating the start of both the back and forward swings. Place a ball on the floor, without a golf club in your hands. Stand in the address position with both knees slightly flexed, weight distributed evenly on both feet and your insteps about shoulder width apart. Now let's go through the movements as outlined next.

- By lifting your left heel, your weight is immediately transferred to your right foot. The left knee becomes free to move, because the weight has been removed from your left leg.
- Your left hip rotates slightly to the right.
- Your left knee moves freely to the right to point just behind the ball, because of movement in your ankle and hip joint. This is where your left knee should point during completion of your backswing.

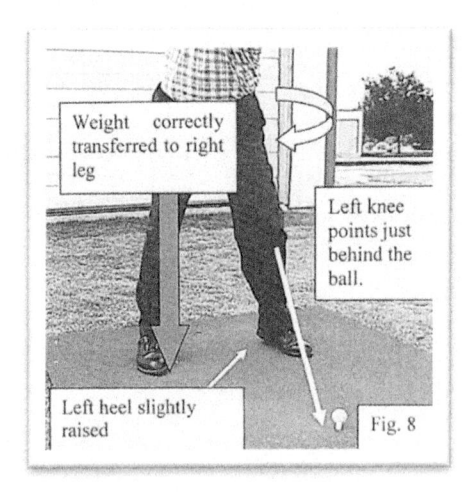

• Your right knee never leaves its slightly flexed position. Almost all your weight (80 – 90 percent) should be on the right leg and foot upon completion of your backswing, as shown in Figure 8.

Weight correctly transferred to right leg
Left knee points just behind the ball.
Left heel slightly raised
Fig. 8

INITIATING YOUR FORWARD SWING CORRECTLY

With a golf club in your hands, and from the position of your completed backswing, do the following:

- Return your *left heel* to the ground while *simultaneously lifting your right heel.* Your weight is immediately transferred to your left foot. The right knee becomes free to move, because the weight has been removed from the right leg.
- Your right hip rotates slightly to the left (Figure 9). Your right knee moves freely to the left to point just ahead of the ball because of movement in your ankle and hip joint. This is where your right knee should point during the initial movement of the forward swing.

- Your left knee should lock into a straight position with no flex in the left knee.

The left and right knee positions are like mirror images.

With your left heel up, your left knee points just behind the ball on the backswing. With your right heel up, your right knee points just in front of the ball on the initial starting of the forward swing.

Fig. 9

PRACTICE

From an address position with your arms at your side, practice these two motions repeatedly—without a club or any arm movements. Get a good feel for initiating the back and forward swings by slightly raising your heels and pointing your knees.

While doing this drill, find a straight line on the floor you can put your toes on. Be sure your back foot is always perpendicular or square to the line. And your forward foot is flared out a little to the left—about 15 degrees. Never stand and practice this drill or swing with both feet flared out; always keep your right foot square to the line. Your forward foot is flared out, so it will be in a better position to support the body when you finish your swing.

TRY THIS EXERCISE

Stand upright, without your golf club, arms hanging at your sides, your knees slightly flexed, facing forward. Place your feet about eight to twelve inches apart. Now turn to the left, with your right hip starting this motion, simultaneously raising your right heel into a vertical position while using the toe of your right shoe as a pivot point. Finish with your head up, looking at your target. All your body weight will be on your left leg while balancing yourself with the right toe.

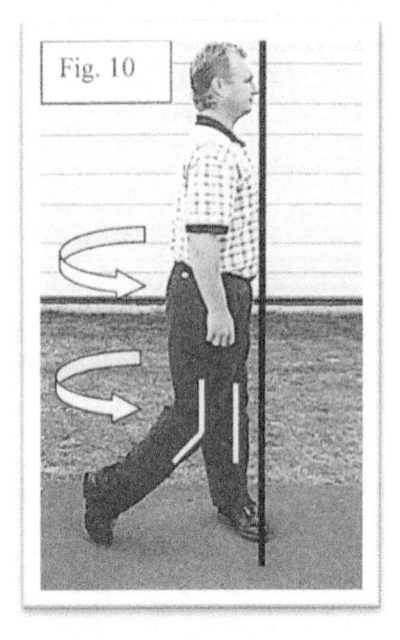

Fig. 10

Concentrate on those movements. You cannot be too quick getting your right heel up! Practice this action until you've got it down and can incorporate this motion into the full swing.

These are the correct lower body movements that you should use in the forward golf swing. Keep your upper body behind the vertical line, as shown in Figure 10. Do not lean the upper body forward slightly bent from the waist where the head and upper body penetrates out beyond the vertical line thus causing your right leg to straighten, pushing the upper body forward.

Now practice swinging with your golf club, being aware of getting your right heel up and the right knee pointing in front of the ball *before* your golf club makes contact.

HOW THE REVERSE WEIGHT SHIFT RELATES TO THE FORWARD SWING

The results of an incorrect forward swing are illustrated in Figure 11. This rigidity in the right leg reverses the hip action, pulls on the back muscles, and forces the left shoulder to the left. All the neck and chest muscles on the left side of the upper body are forced into tension, thus pulling the head up and left. At this point, you normally lose your balance and fall backward or step to the left.

Lower right leg rigid with weight thrust onto it during the forward swing

Fig. 11

Your golfing friend will say, *"You looked up. Keep your head down."* As shown here, with the next swing you try harder to keep your head down, but this exacerbates the problem with the right leg by forcing the weight to totally remain on your right side. The result is that you hit behind the ball, or you pull the ball dead left, or you have no follow-through, or you step to the left with your right foot anchored to the ground.

If your fellow golfer sees the club coming across your body harshly, and you have to step to the left, he may say, *"You tried to kill it!"* From that point on, every time this happens, even years later, you have the misconception that you tried to kill it or you swung too fast. You work on everything trying to correct your swing faults except raising and turning your right heel.

Now you know differently.

The reverse weight shift is the most common problem of golfers. The reverse shift causes a person to fall off balance and forces the head up. The poor right leg is just trying to do what it does naturally—to stay rigid while supporting the body.

What is the key to prevent these problems?

KEY TO A SMOOTH SWING

Simultaneously, lift your right heel; and rotate your right hip and right shoulder to the left. This one move is the hardest thing to execute in the golf swing! Why?

You cannot perform a smooth golf swing
if your right heel cannot lift.

You will be unable to shift your weight to the left leg and complete the follow-through. This is the key to a smooth, fluid golf swing. The finished follow-through is correctly illustrated in Figure 12.

- Let your right heel kick up to the right, keeping your right knee slightly flexed to finish next to your left knee.
- This motion happens while your right hip rotates to the left. The rotation of your right foot and flexed knee eliminates any tension, allowing you to keep the club head on target, finishing your follow-through.

Fig. 12

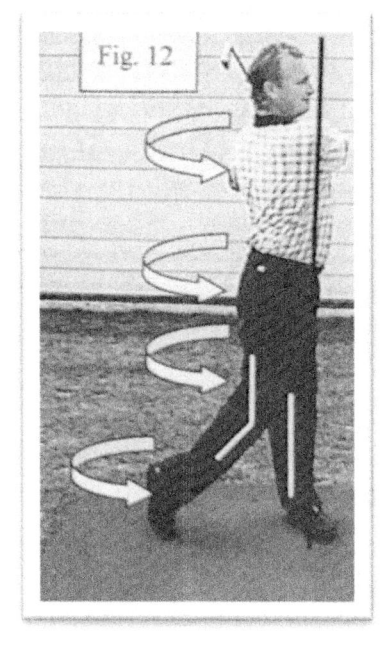

- Any tension or straightening of your right knee at the finish of the swing will push your upper body ahead of the black line, resulting in lost distance.
- At the finish of the follow-through, you will be standing on your left leg, facing the target, in balance, head up, looking down the fairway, not at the ground.

Many golfers practice swinging using poor swing movements. While practicing their swing, they don't use their heels or legs. They are still looking at the ground on their follow-through. They should be doing just the opposite by using their heels and legs and looking up at their target upon completion of the practice swing.

KEEP YOUR HEAD STEADY, NOT DOWN

Do not keep your head down while you practice swinging or after striking the ball in a real swing.

I repeat, do not keep your head down!

Keeping your head down too long during your follow through will restrict your follow-through, and you will pull the ball to the left of your target. Imagine the golf swing as a wooden spoke wagon wheel. Your head would be the hub of the wheel. Imagine that the hub of the wheel doesn't start turning forward until you contact the ball with the club head. Keep your head steady as you swing around it or until you've hit the ball! On the forward swing and after contact with the ball, this is the swing sequence.

- Your arms will start to pull your head up after they reach full extension about waist high.
- Let this steady natural pulling motion from your arms as they rotate your head up and into a finished position until you're looking down the fairway at your target.

Always try to swing past your own head into the finish of the swing—*just let the ball get in the way.* Some golfers swing at the ball and when they make contact, they stop their swing without realizing it. Don't stop swinging after you hit the ball! *Swing to the completion of the follow-through every time.*

There are golfers who vary from good golf swing basics and still hit a golf ball well. They hit the ball without using any leg action or while standing flat-footed. You can do it but your potential of longer distance and accuracy is somewhat limited from these positions. When you watch the professional golfers on TV, watch the basic leg and head action; you will not see them looking at the ground when they have completed their swing. They will be standing in balance on their left leg, their right toe as a pivot point and with their arms in a completed follow through, looking down the fairway at the target. If when they finish their swing and they are looking down the fairway, they must of moved their heads. Do not keep your head down.

THE MAJOR DIFFERENCE BETWEEN THE LEFT KNEE AND RIGHT KNEE

Fig. 13

In Figures 13 and 14, we can see one of the major differences between your left and right knee positions. The difference is in your right leg from the point where your right knee points in front of the ball forward to the completion of the forward swing. During the swing, your right leg, weight off, rotates and follows the movement of your right hip, using the toe of the foot as a pivot point. Kick your right heel up into a vertical position. Be sure you complete the follow through head up, facing down the fairway.

If this is difficult to do, then you are lifting your right heel only part way and not quickly enough. Flip the right heel up to the right into a vertical position as you turn to the left. If you achieve the vertical position, it will be much easier to turn your body.

Don't try to make an unnatural move with your knees sideways or laterally in the bottom part of the swing. This unnatural action will block the rotation of the right leg, not allowing your heel to freely kick up to the right, while forcing some weight to remain on the right leg while swinging.

As in walking, remember the main function of the knee is to move straight forward and back to its natural position. Allow your right hip—as it rotates left—to pull your right leg through the golf swing. Using the natural movement of the legs will remove stress on back muscles, hip joints and both knee joints.

Knee, hip joints and back muscles hurt when your body tries to rotate to the left and you finish your swing with weight on your back leg. You want to use your legs naturally, as you do when you're walking. Transferring your weight from one leg to the other is something we do thousands of times a day without thinking. The instant you raise one of your heels your weight is on the other foot naturally. Flex should only be in your right knee and no flex in your left knee when the swing finishes. As shown in Figure 14, your left leg should be totally straight with at least 90-100 percent of your weight on your left or forward leg, keeping your upper body behind the vertical line or over your left leg with your belt buckle against the line when finished.

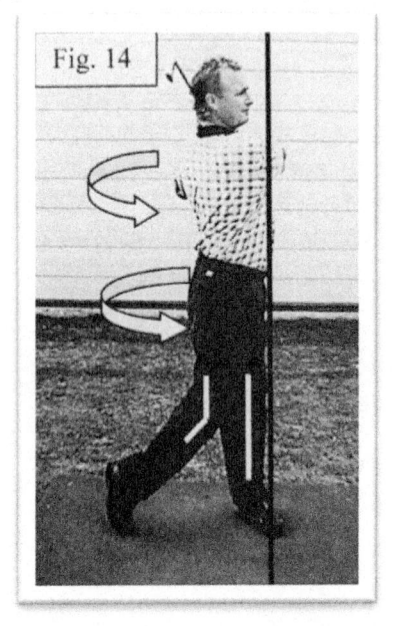

The golfing result of poor leg action is a too fast, topped, looked up, fat, pulled, sliced, bailout kill shot, or something worse!

But…

With a little practice these motions with your legs will bring back your flexibility and swing speed. The ball will go farther without you trying to swing harder. Also, these motions will reduce hip, backache and knee pain.

THE LOWER BODY EXECUTES THE
START OF THE FORWARD SWING

The following is a main reason golfers top the golf ball: the hands and club in the forward swing get ahead of your back leg action resulting in a topped golf ball. Otherwise, the right foot, with the additional weight on it, is still sitting on the ground as your hands and club in the forward swing passes through, ahead of the leg action.

How do you know if you're starting your lower body action soon enough? Here is a test you can use throughout your golfing life.

Now, set up in a hitting address position with a seven iron and no ball. Swing your seven-iron in a complete backswing and then forward swing to a complete finish with your head up and on the toe of your right foot looking at your target not down at the floor. Hold that finish for at least to a count of three, then from the finished position swing back through to the full back swing and back to the finish again holding to the count of three. Repeat this swinging action for three continuous swings without stopping to reset the golf club at the address position.

On each forward swing, did you feel the club brush or hear it touch the ground? If you did not hear or feel the club touching the ground, then your upper body is trying to do all the work and is starting the forward swing from the top of your swing. You are getting ahead of your lower body. The initial movements of your right heel and knee in the start of the forward swing will allow the golf club head to keep coming at the ball and touch the ground.

Keep trying three easy swings without stopping, as shown in Figure 15. Keep starting the right hip and leg quicker and quicker until you feel or hear the club brush the ground on each forward swing.

For the rest of your golfing life, you can use this test.

Remember, if you don't feel or hear the club brush the ground, it means your upper body is starting the forward swing and getting ahead of your lower body. You know your swing timing is correct if you can hear and feel the club brush the ground on each repetition.

If you realize you did something wrong during this swinging drill, such as keeping your head down, don't stop and reset the club at the bottom of the swing. I repeat don't stop and reset the club at the bottom of the swing and start over. If your right heel didn't make it to a vertical position on your second swing, correct it on your next swing without starting over.

Finish each swing with your right toe as a pivot point, your head up, looking at your target, and your upper body over your left leg in good balance.

At the finish of your follow-through, do not let your upper body lean out ahead of the lower part of your left leg. Imagine a straight line from the outside of your left foot pointing skyward (Figure 14). Always keep your upper body behind the line. Finish standing with your body weight directly over a straight left leg with no flex in the left knee. Relaxing your right knee will help.

WHY YOU WANT TO KEEP SWINGING BACK AND FORTH WITHOUT STOPPING

There is a reason for continuing the swing without resetting the club. By resetting the club at the bottom each time you make a swing error, you create confusion between your mind and body.
- I was still looking at the ground when I finished my swing, oops, you reset the club and you start over.
- I didn't start with my right hip, oops, you reset the club and you start over.

- My weight was still on my right leg, oops, you reset the club and you start over.

Let's say you were going to read a book the same way. The first line in the book is, *"The dog bit the little boy."*
The dog (oops, you start over.)
The dog bit (oops, you start over.)
The dog bit the (oops, you start over.)

Imagine reading the whole book this way. You can see the confusion this creates between your mind and body in trying to learn your new swing task. Continue your easy swings without stopping, so your mind and body can learn all the swing tasks together without confusion.

Especially, take three swings at the driving range between each ball.

HINT: Over analysis of each movement causes paralysis!

Your lower body motion is the starter engine that dictates reactions and/or movements of your upper body. The lower right side of your body is the starter button for your forward swing.

The lower body will pull your upper body into the ball striking area. The feeling of this movement is almost like the movements you make in skipping rocks on the water. Your right elbow will ride close to your hip with a slight sidearm motion. Your arms will feel like they're dropping into the ball striking area.

Wind up the body swing from the top down to the feet.

Unwind the body swing from the bottom up to the head.

THE PROPER WIDTH IN THE STANCE AND DISTANCE FROM THE BALL

In Figures 16 and 17, let's look at the stance while we are correcting the lower body. Put your feet about six inches apart. Start a full backswing. You will feel your weight roll to the outer edge of your right foot. If your stance is too narrow, the weight on the outside edge of your right foot will make it difficult to start the forward swing. Now, take a really extra wide stance. If your stance is too wide, even though you raise your left heel, your weight will not transfer fully to your right leg.

Find a stance that when you start to take your full backswing, and as your left heel clears the ground, you find your weight on the right foot evenly distributed. Just as when you're walking, the body likes the total weight distributed evenly on the foot.

It's better if your weight is just slightly on the instep of your right foot and not rolling to the outside.

A GREAT SWING DRILL TO PRACTICE A LOT

I'm going to insert a great swing drill here that you can do inside when it's cold, raining or dark out and you have no place to swing.

As in Figure 18, place a ball or tin can lid on the floor. To determine the proper distance, you should stand back from the ball at address, and place a five iron on the floor with the ball at the hosel of the club—where the shaft enters the club head. Now, place your feet straddling the shaft of the club. Place your toes, where the shaft of the club meets the grip, about eight inches from the grip end of the club. Place your left instep about one to two inches to the left of the shaft. Place your right foot at a point right of the shaft, wide enough for your right leg to receive your full body weight during a backswing.

Now bend over and pick up the club. Place the club behind the small of your back, with the grip end to your left, as shown in Figure 19. The club is held in a horizontal position behind your back using your arms in the crooks of your elbows, in prisoner position.

Hold your hands and lower arms waist high, elbows by your sides, with your lower arms pointing straight out in front of you. Keep your hands in a relaxed vertical position with your palms facing each other. This set up works with any club. Flex your knees slightly. You should feel like you are just beginning to sit down on a stool. Keep your head and shoulders up, knees flexed and in a good golf stance. The stance should be as wide as previously discussed.

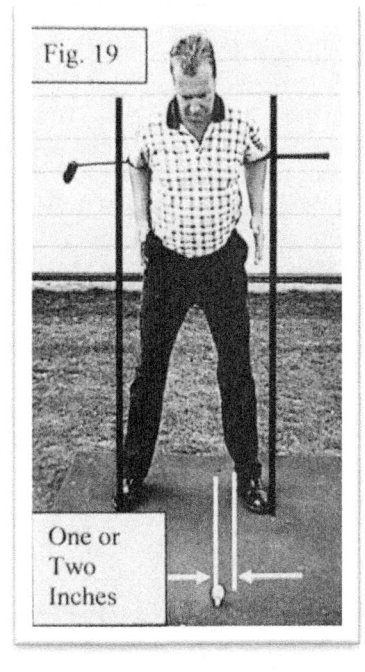

Fig. 19

One or Two Inches

Without dipping or raising up, imagine staying between the vertical lines as shown in Figure 20 and start your backswing.

1. Rotate your left hip and shoulder. Do this while lifting your left heel and pointing your left knee just behind the ball. Not too steep, with the left shoulder flatter like a baseball swing. Visualize keeping your left arm pit above the ball.

Fig. 20

2. Let your left shoulder rotate under your chin until the club grip points well above the top of the ball. See the dashed white arrow line.

3. Your back should be facing down the fairway.

4. The flex in your right knee should remain there throughout the back swing.

Fig. 21

Now, start the forward swing.

1. Returning your left heel to the ground, raise your right heel simultaneously with your right hip and shoulder movements as discussed before, and as shown in Figure 21.

2. Turn your body to the left until you point the head of the club above the top of the ball.

3. You should be standing on your left leg with your head up, upper body over the left leg, looking down the fairway, as shown in Figure 22.

30

Using your heels properly will keep your head steady as you start your backswing and forward swing. Lifting your heels will keep you from bobbing up and down or moving side to side and not rotating your body.

Look in the mirror—make sure your head and upper body are not bobbing. Keeping your head steady, make sure you are rotating your body until your left shoulder is around and under your chin. Also, make sure you are rotating the body and not just moving it laterally. Finish every swing with your head up and facing down the fairway.

With the club held behind your back, take the backswing again to its completion, pointing the club grip above the ball. Remove the club from behind your back while holding your body in position. Move your arms and club up to the top of the backswing, putting the club in your hands above your head and over your right shoulder. Your wrist should be cocked. This position will be the same position as at the end of a full backswing.

Fig. 22

Now, with the club behind your back, do just the opposite for the forward swing. Finish with your head up, as if facing down the fairway, as shown in Figures 21 and 22. Hold that position and remove the club from behind your back. Move your arms and club to the top of the follow-through with your wrist cocked. Place the club over your left shoulder, as shown in Figure 23. This position is the same as your full golf swing — weight on left foot, balance maintained by right toe, head up and looking down the fairway just past your arms.

Your hands and forearms always finish over your left shoulder, hands away from your head for balance. Do not finish your golf swing, with your hands next to your head.

Your hands, when finishing close to your head, will cause you to lose your balance and make you fall forward or be in the way to where you can't properly finish the swing in balance.

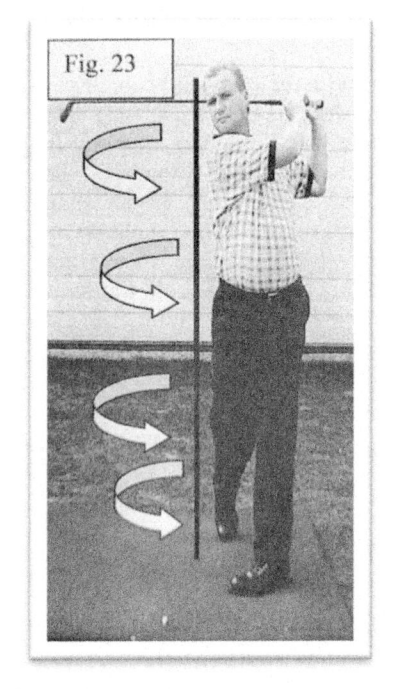

In Figure 24, we see the arms for the first time at full extension. The head will be pulled up by the arms, starting at this point in your swing and continue to the finish.

Notice that with the club behind your back, your hands are passive in this drill. By passive I mean they are not doing anything. They are not starting your backswing or forward swing. The same holds true while swinging the golf club. Other parts of the body initiate the swing.

With the club behind your back in a full completed backswing with the grip pointing just above the ball, have someone grab the club grip and tell them not to let the grip move forward towards the target. As you slowly start to rotate forward with your right heel, hip and shoulder, you will notice a lot of force comes from your body rotation. Your helper may not be able to keep the club handle from moving.

Your hands should remain passive; they do not start the forward swing. Also, you will feel the strength in the swing coming from the lower body and shoulders as your helper keeps the grip of the club from moving forward. This is the move that starts the forward swing. Momentum from the rotation of the body brings the shoulders, arms, hands and club head into the ball striking area at a terrific speed.

Fig. 24

The ball striking area on the forward swing arc is from waist or hip high to the back of the ball. The arms come to a stop at the completion of the back swing at the point of changing direction and then start forward from zero miles per hour. During the forward swing, the arms are constantly increasing in speed until they reach the maximum at the ball. They don't start the forward swing at the maximum.

Notice in this swing drill with the club behind your back that your back and forward swings are only as fast as your body rotates your shoulders. It's not as fast as your arms and hands would like to go. Use this same tempo while swinging the golf club.

Use this drill for warming up and before hitting practice balls or teeing off. Let your shoulders dictate your swing speed. Never warm up with this drill, finishing looking at the ground flat footed; always use your heels, finishing head up on your right toe for balance.

KEEP YOUR HEAD AND SHOULDERS UP EVEN IF YOU WEAR GLASSES

Even if you wear glasses, be sure to keep your head and shoulders up. Don't bend over to look over your bifocals or trifocals, even if the ball looks fuzzy. Your head position will be too low. A low head and shoulder position, as shown in Figure 25, will not allow your left shoulder to rotate under your chin. This causes a down force on your left leg, thus restricting your shoulder turn. It does not allow you to complete a full fluid backswing and forces your arms to take over the start of the forward swing. Other results are reverse weight shift, and arms forced out of the swing plane.

As in Figure 25, let's say you were in this address position, and I was standing five or six feet in front of you. By raising your eyes only and not your head, how much of me could you see? From past experience, most people can't see above my ankles.

After you have placed the club behind the ball at address, your head should be positioned, as shown in Figure 26. You should look at the ball by looking down just past your cheekbones. Then, by raising your eyes only, you should be able to look a person in the face, who is standing five or six feet in front of you. You can also try this indoors by looking at yourself in a mirror. If you can only see your ankles or waist, your head and shoulders are positioned too low. You must start over, stand up and reposition the club, and keep your head and shoulders up.

If you just raise your head, without starting over, your head will move up but your shoulders will not move up. Your shoulders will remain in a low incorrect position.

This low head and shoulder position will cause tension in your left shoulder turn. Restriction will be forcing your upper body to put a down force on your left leg restricting a proper weight shift from left leg to right leg, even if you raise your left heel.

Fig. 26

By raising your eyes only, you should be able to look a person in the face.

A PARTING SHOT ON THE LOWER BODY

Remember that a swing based on good posture never changes, but poor posture will constantly change your swing.

*Good posture, good swing, no tension,
no restriction, and no pain.*

As you have read, and with your help, we have eliminated a lot of the things on the list at the start of this book. You have learned that every day, the right leg forces thousands of golfers out of a good golf shot. The reverse weight shift onto the right leg also puts all kinds of stress on the body.

If you lack the proper leg movements:

- You feel like you lack flexibility, with no backswing and no follow-through.
- You have a back or knees that hurt when you play golf.
- You think you are too old to take a full backswing.
- You look like you tried to kill it or swung too fast.
- You look like you looked up.
- You are forced up and out of the golf shot.

Everybody should start the forward swing with the lower body simultaneously with the upper body. Lift and rotate your right heel on the forward swing. This will get the weight off your right leg and eliminate a lot of inconsistency in your golf game.

It is possible to hit a ball from almost any position: on your knees, blind folded or one handed. I would urge you to stay close to the basics, which is just using the natural body movements in the golf swing. Watch good golfers and the professional golfers on TV during tournaments. If they thought they could shoot lower scores and make money playing on one foot while blindfolded, believe me, they would! Those professionals are out there making a living at this game. Mimic them as much as possible. You will not see a professional complete a full swing keeping his head down or looking at the ground. Pros complete their swings, head up and looking down the fairway or at their target. They do this by using proper leg action.

CHAPTER TWO
How to Grip the Club

This chapter will address the grip. I am going to give you the basics or standards set through years of experience by players. The professionals on tour use these basics. They may vary slightly, but none will stray too far.

Having the proper grip will enhance your ability to strike the ball solidly and hit it farther.

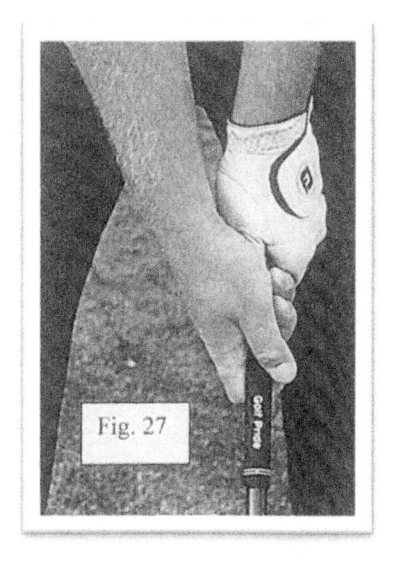

Fig. 27

There are several important basics to the grip. One, get the butt of the club under the pad or heel of your left hand; two, get your right hand behind the club.

PLACING THE CLUB UNDER THE HEEL
OF THE LEFT HAND FOR BETTER GRIP

Reach out with your left arm straight and at shoulder height. Take hold of the grip in your fist, pressing the end of the club against the heel of your left hand with the shaft of the club square up across your finger points, where the fingers meet the palm of your hand. As in Figure 28, hold the golf club in a straight up position with the shaft of the club pointing skyward and the tip of the club head pointing toward you.

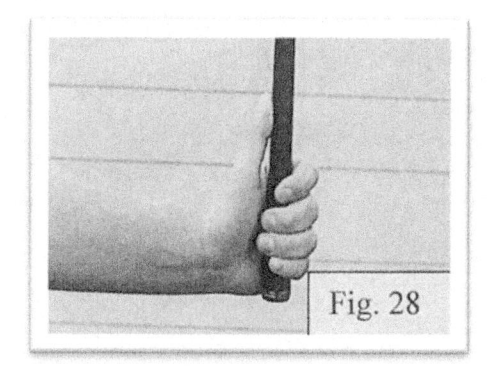

Fig. 28

Be sure the club grip is under the heel of your left hand. Thumb right of the logo or center of the club. You should see two or three knuckles.

Hold the club in your fingers with the butt of the club under the heel of your hand. Your thumb points toward the club head, placed slightly on the right side of the shaft. You will be looking at the top or narrow side of your wrist with a slight canter to the right. Most of the gripping pressure will be with the last three fingers of the left hand.

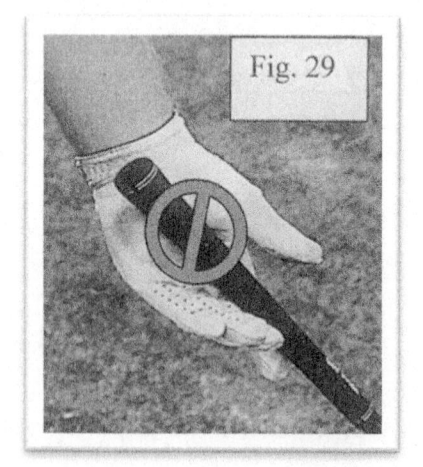

While standing straight up and gripping the club, as shown in Figure 28, tip the head of the golf club forward until it's pointing straight out in front of you with the tip of the club head pointing skyward. *Without bending your elbow,* you should be able to cock the club from straight out to straight up.

Fig. 29

Do not set the club shaft in the center of your left hand, left of the heel or in the fat part of the palm, as shown in Figure 29. If you hold the club in this position, it will do one of two things: Either move the grip of the left hand too far to the left or too far to the right on top of the club shaft. Mainly, the club held in either position will inhibit a natural wrist cocking action and inhibit a good hand position at the top of the backswing.

Now, another way to obtain the proper left hand grip, as shown in Figures 29 A, B and C, is to start by holding an iron golf club horizontally in your left hand across your body, with the club head resting in your right hand, clubhead face lying flat with the groves of the club face facing skyward.

Simultaneously, grip the club handle with a straight left arm, left hand gripping, with the club grip under the heal of your left hand. Place your left thumb pointing down the club shaft just right of the grip logo and not in the center on the logo, as shown in Figure 29 C.

Do not raise your left wrist while gripping with your left hand. Do not place the club in the center of your hand but in the fingers and under the heal of the palm. While gripping with your left hand, keep your left wrist down in a natural position, because if you raise your wrist above the horizontal, you will not obtain the proper grip (Figure 29).

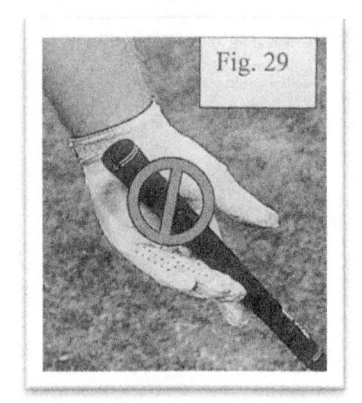

Fig. 29

Now while maintaining your grip with the left hand and before you place your right hand on the club, place the club head behind the golf ball. Again, if your club looks closed, do not change your grip before placing the right hand grip on the club. Just roll your left arm slightly to the right until the club face is facing straight at the target. Then place your right hand and properly grip the club shaft.

Fig 29D

Now with the completed grip, try cocking and uncocking the left wrist. There should be no tension preventing your left wrist from cocking freely in the backswing. This sequence can be used while practicing or before you hit the ball during your golf round. It only takes a couple of seconds to get your grip with a little practice. Your left thumb should always be lying just right of the logo on the center of the club grip, and you should see about two to three knuckles of your left hand when looking down at your hands at the address position.

Another way, each club has a balance point usually a few inches up the shaft from the club head, as in Figure 29 D. Hold the 8-iron horizontal, high above your head, with two fingers of your right hand at the balance point—toe of club pointing at the ground, and your left hand thumb again down the shaft, arms straight above your head. Without looking up, feel the grip under the heel of your left hand. Bring the club down to a normal position with your left hand. Notice, your thumb should be right of the center logo and under the heel of your hand, as shown in Figure 30. Figure 30 shows the correct left hand position. A club held correctly in the left hand will let your wrist cock and un-cock naturally throughout the swing.

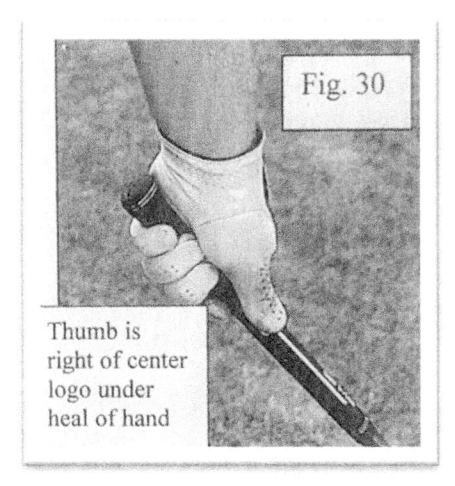

Fig. 30

Thumb is right of center logo under heal of hand

This grip will increase your club head speed, distance and ball striking. You will be able to get rid of the weak golf shots out to the right with no distance. Or the need to turn your body so quickly to the left, just to square up a weak club head position in the hitting area.

PLACING AND GRIPPING WITH THE RIGHT HAND

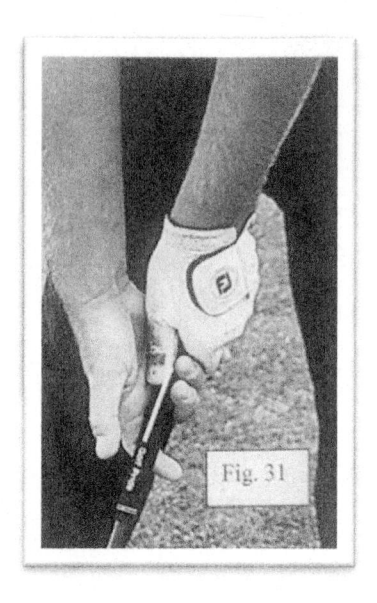

While keeping your right elbow touching your right hip, place your right hand out in front of you with the palm slightly up in a cupping position, like reaching out to shake hands. Keep all four fingers together with your thumb raised and about an inch above your index finger. Now, as shown in Figures 30 and 31, place the palm of your right hand over the left thumb. While looking down, you will see the cupped palm of your right hand is directly opposite of and covering your large thumb joint of your left hand. Your little finger will wrap over the knuckle of your left index finger, as shown in Figures 32 and 33. The two middle fingers of your right hand will be on the grip of the club, and your thumb and index finger will encircle the club.

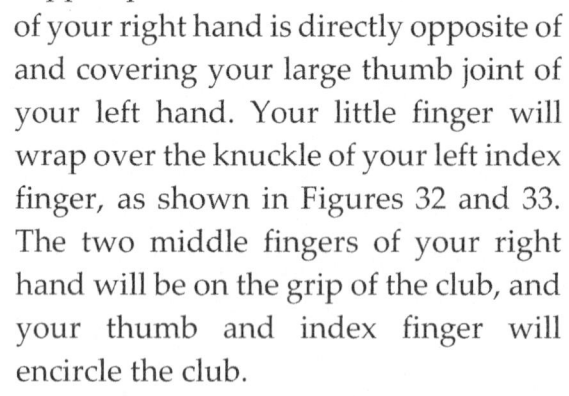

NOTE: To keep from getting a sore left hand, be sure the middle fingers of your right hand are on the club and not up on the skin of the left hand.

Fig. 34 - INTERLOCK

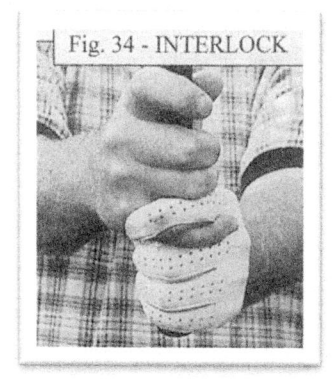

Some golfers prefer to use the interlocking grip as shown in Figure 34. But if neither grip feels comfortable to you, simplify the procedure by grabbing the grip like a baseball bat with all ten fingers wrapped around the club.

Just remember to keep the club under the heel of the left hand and the right hand behind the shaft.

PLACING THE RIGHT HAND BEHIND THE SHAFT

Let's say you are pounding a nail into a tree just about thigh high. You would grab the hammer with your right hand and swing sideways at the nail with your right hand behind the handle of the hammer, your elbow close to your body.

You wouldn't drive a nail with a straight arm. You would not place your hand on the hammer with the head of the hammer pointing at the nail and your palm of your right hand pointing at the ground. Also, you would not have the palm of your right hand pointing skyward.

It's the same way when placing the right hand on the club: Your right palm faces the golf ball.

When addressing the ball, imagine that your right arm is longer and extends right down to the ball, as shown in Figure 35.

When striking the ball with the golf club, you want the feeling of hitting the ball right in the center of the palm of your right hand.

Hold out two fingers of your left hand. With your fingertips, tap the center of your right hand palm. This is where you want to hit the ball. Visualize that your right hand is just behind the shaft and ball. Visualize striking the ball right in the center of your palm the same as you would pound a nail thigh high into a tree with a hammer.

Fig. 35

I want to inject something here that goes along with the grip and leg action.

The right elbow should be close to your side. Put your elbow against your right side, your forearm pointing straight out from you with palm open and facing the target. Feel the right elbow close to your side while chipping or swinging to prevent shanking the golf ball to the right.

The swing is a two-handed game: The left hand is giving you the depth of the swing and leading the swing, while the right hand increases the power and stability. The right elbow adds additional club speed; like throwing a ball, the elbow acts like a lever. Without it, you can't throw a fast ball.

While delivering the power, sometimes we grip so fiercely with a weak left hand grip (club in the palm of the left hand) that the wrist action is prohibited to hinge and unhinge effortlessly. This leaves the clubface open. It is so open that the shaft of the club—where it goes into the club head (hosel)—hits the ball before the clubface. The result is a ball going dead right instead of forward. This shot is called a shank. If this starts happening, check your right hand position and grip pressure. Make sure the right hand is behind the shaft and the right elbow is close to your side.

There are a lot of ugly words in golf. Some would say the ugliest word is SHANK!!!!!!!!!

Relax the death grip of the left hand, equalizing the grip by increasing the grip with the right hand. Try hitting the ball more in the center of the right hand palm, right elbow close to your side, left hand hinging on the take away and leading on the forward stroke. Right and left hands rolling from right to left through the hitting area.

Normal grip pressure is about 55 percent in the last three fingers of the left hand and 45 percent in the middle two fingers of the right hand. However, I want you to grip 60 percent with the right hand and 40 percent with the left.

Also, to keep from shanking the ball to the right, make sure your leg and foot movements are correct. That means turning your body and not sliding or moving slightly forward into the ball. For leg and foot movements, see Chapter One.

CHAPTER THREE
Ball Position, Stance and Set Up

You previously learned how far to stand from the ball, and how far the ball should be from the toes of your feet, while placing the ball at the hosel of the club, where the shaft goes into the head of the club. As you straddle the shaft, your toes are placed where the shaft meets the grip of the club. This will be about the right distance from the ball.

From a set up position, let your arms hang down in a relaxed position, with the club set up behind the ball. You should not reach out bending the body too much from the waist, nor should you be too upright with your hands too close to your body. There should be about a fist width from your body to the butt of the club and your hands.

Looking straight on at Figure 36, you can see the ball is played about an inch or two inside the left heel or instep. The ball is always played like it's sitting on the left cheek of your face. What this means is that if you picked the ball straight up, the backside of the ball would line up with and be touching your left cheek. This always puts your head behind the ball.

Imagine a cut out of your head being flat as a pancake and placed on the ground face up, directly behind the ball. The ball would line up with the left side of your face, with your head totally behind the ball.

Your hands are always placed between the tip of your left shoulder and the left side of your face.

Fig. 37

THE STANCE AND ADDRESS POSITION

As shown in Figure 37, place a club on the ground, club head and shaft pointing at the flag or target. Stand the correct distance from the ball and place a second club parallel to the first club, right at the tip of your toes. Place your right foot at a perpendicular or right angle to the club. Place your left toe angled slightly to the left.

Imagine standing on the green and aiming or lining the club head right behind the flag at the base, as shown in Figure 38. If you took the same stance, as shown in Figure 37, your toe line would be the same distance from the flag as it was when addressing the ball.

These lines are parallel like railroad tracks. The width varies between the two lines, because you have longer and shorter clubs. They are always parallel to each other and perpendicular to your right foot, as shown in Figures 37 and 38.

Your stance will change somewhat with your selection of irons. The stance is square with a five iron, both tips of your shoes touching the toe line and your right foot perpendicular to the target line. Keep your shoulders and knees lined up with the toe line.

Evenly distribute your weight between your heels and the balls of the feet. For iron shots, your body weight should be placed 50 percent on the left foot and 50 percent on the right foot. For metal wood shots, place 40 percent of your weight on the left foot and 60 percent on the right foot.

As you change to a more lofted club or shorter clubs, start moving the left foot only away from the toe line. This is to open up your left hip on the forward swing.

If your stance is closed with shorter clubs (left foot ahead of the right foot), thus because of the shorter swing, the left hip and foot will block the turning of the forward swing. This will cause a pull to the left and/or block the shot to the right. Also, it will restrict your follow through. This closed stance is shown in Figure 39.

With a short club, imagine that your clubface is facing the pitcher's mound and your left foot is pulled back towards the third base line. Try to hit the ball over second base. When you open your stance, it looks like the ball is being played back in your stance. If you just lean back on your heels and rotate your left foot back to 90 degrees, you will see that the ball is actually being played just inside your left instep by two to three inches.

Remember to keep your knees and shoulders parallel to the target line, like railroad tracks. Don't take your stance with your shoulders, knees, feet and clubface aimed at the same target, as in Figure 39.

Always aim your shoulders and toe line left of the flag the same distance you would be from the flag and toes of your feet, as if you were standing on the green with the club in your hands and the club head at the flag. Unless you were hitting a fade or draw then you would move your target left or right, keeping your feet parallel to the club head line to the new target.

Fig. 39

SET UP ROUTINE

All good golfers have a set up routine when they address the ball.

1. Choose a line to the target while standing several yards behind the ball.

2. Pick out a mark several feet in front of the ball in line with the target.

3. Simultaneously:
   - Place your right hand behind the club.
   - Place the club behind the ball, aiming the club face at your target.
   - Place your right foot first at 90 degrees or perpendicular to your target line.

Never place your right or back foot with the toe flared out to the right, always 90 degrees to the target line.

4. Place your left foot with the toe a little flared to the left, so that the ball is aligned at an inch or two inside your left heel. Always place your left foot slightly flared left, after the right foot.

5. Complete the gripping of the club with both hands.

6. Keep your hands and forearms relaxed and in motion (This is called waggling).

7. Look at the mark several feet in front of the ball and then to the target.

8. Give yourself several seconds to let your subconscious set all the muscles into motion.

9. Make the full golf swing, swinging through the ball and not just striking at the ball.

This is just one routine. There are others that are similar. Most good golfers will stand behind the ball, look at the target and pick a point several feet in front of the ball. They will use that spot to line up on the target, keeping their knees, hips and shoulders parallel to the target line. Imagine the rails on a railroad track and place the club head on one rail and your toes up against the other rail.

Fig. 40

NEVER PLACE YOUR LEFT FOOT FIRST

<u>*DO NOT*</u> address the ball by setting your left foot down first. This will set your hips and shoulders in a closed position. Your hips, shoulders, knees and feet will be aimed right of a

line parallel to the target line. As in Figure 40, you will be lined up to the right trying to hit the ball towards your target which will be left of your body alignment. This bad alignment (left hip blocking the forward swing) and will cause numerous problems: Swinging from the top, pulling the ball left, enhancing a slice, and a strain on the body are just a few.

Always place your right foot first and always keep it at 90 degrees. This goes for a full shot, chipping and putting. This is a big problem with many golfers, stepping up to the ball with the club in their hand with the left foot first.

Always place the right foot first.

YOU CAN TEST THIS FOR YOURSELF

Pick out a target and then take your stance by placing your left foot first. Bend over and place a club across your toes. Step back and see if your toe line is parallel to your clubface line and left of your target by the length of the club you are using. Or is the toe line club on the ground pointing right of your original target putting your stance in a closed position? Now do the same thing, but place your right foot first at address. Your clubface should be in line with the target line and your toe line left of the target, parallel to the clubface line—see Figure 38.

Here is an exception: Address the ball with your feet together side by side. This will line up your hips and shoulders parallel to the ball and your imaginary target line you have picked out to the target. From this position only—with your feet together and your hips and shoulders in line left of your target—place your left foot first and then your right foot.

CHAPTER FOUR
Upper Body

There are lots of parts to the upper body that affect your swing. They include hands, arms, shoulders, torso, neck, head and all the internal parts, including our computer, the brain.

CONSTANT SHOULDER PLANE

Have you ever seen a swing testing machine to test golf clubs? If you have, you would know that the swing testing machine has no head or shoulders. If the swing test machine had a head and shoulders, the head would be above the line from the "head of the golf club" to where the "handle of the golf club" is attached to the machine arm.

The golf club, the arm which is that part of the machine to which the golf club is attached, and the steel plate supporting the whole mechanical mechanism are on the same swing plane. The machine, as it cocks the club back and releases through, *maintains the same swing plane.* It uses the same swing plane for both the backswing and the forward swing.

From the address position, the head and shoulders (from the underarms up) stay above the swing plane line throughout backswing and the forward swing. It is just like the swing machine.

Let's start by understanding and using a constant shoulder plane in your golf swing.

Try this.

As shown in Figure 41, take a normal stance and put a driver in your left hand and a three-metal wood in your right hand. Hang onto the head of the clubs, with the grips pointing about two inches above the ball. Visualize a straight line running from the ball, along the bottom of the club shafts to your underarms and right through your body. Keep the clubs shoulder width apart.

Slowly, start a *partial backswing* by rotating your body and shoulders to the right. Keep the club in your left hand pointing and moving just above the ball. *Visualize* this swing plane as the grip passes over the top of the ball.

58

Now, slowly rotate to the left through the hitting area. Keep the club grip in your right and left hand pointing above the ball. *Visualize* keeping this swing plane from the beginning to a completed backswing, and also on the forward swing to the completed follow through. Do not allow either underarm to drop down below the white line. This shoulder plane will produce a slight draw, moving the ball in flight from right to left.

In Figure 43, you can see both the beginning of and the completed backswing. In both, keep your underarms above the white line. By visualizing, you get the feeling that your underarms are just about touching the top of the golf ball as they pass over.

Fig. 43

CHECK YOUR SHOULDER PLANE

After hitting a few balls at the driving range, you should first check that you have the proper alignment and leg action. Then, check your shoulder swing plane.

Let's say the first two or three range balls you hit are fading or slicing. The ball moves from left to right. You are also digging deep divots in the ground. You don't have to hit a bucket of balls to work it out. The first thought you should have is that your right shoulder plane is too steep coming into the hitting area.

Too steep means that while swinging, the shoulder plane line is pointing somewhere between the golf ball and the tip of your toes.

The dashed lines in Figure 44 depict a steep shoulder plane. A steep right shoulder plane will force your hips quickly to the left and give you a feeling that your lower body is sliding forward. This doesn't allow you to physically close the clubface and causes you to push and fade the ball to the right. Some would tell you the problem is hanging on too long with the left hand. Flatten out your shoulder swing by visually aiming your underarms (both left and right) higher above the ball (white line) until you start drawing the ball. This will eliminate the shoulder plane swing problems. Let's try to simplify this process a little more.

Visualization is the key to a proper swing plane.

Look again at the white lines in the Figures 41 through 44. These lines represent the shoulder planes for both the *backswing and forward swing*. When you start your backswing, you should visualize having your left underarm passing above the ball. When your right shoulder is on the forward swing, visualize having your right underarm passing above the ball.

While you're swinging, you simply visualize aiming your underarms both left and right at the top of the golf ball, as depicted in the pictures. You keep aiming a little higher until you start drawing the ball slightly to the left.

Through my teaching experience, I have found that most golfers by steeping their shoulder swing plane the slightest, go from aiming their underarms at the top of the ball (12 o'clock) to aiming at the bottom of the ball (6 o'clock). They go from hitting a draw (slightly left) to hitting a fade (slightly right).

NATURAL AIMING METHOD FOR THE SHOULDER PLANE

Like aiming a rifle, this will give you a natural aiming device to put your shoulders on the proper plane. Each person may vary slightly but, with a little practice, using aiming, you will visualize and find your best shoulder swing plane.

Through imagination, the mind can take aim at an object without any physical pointer.

You can raise your right arm and point at something with your index finger. You can also imagine your right arm rising and pointing without actually physically doing it. That's because of our brain and eyesight physically work in combination. We can see the golf ball teed up in front of us. We can imagine, during our backswing, that if we draw a line from our left underarm to the top of the ball, we could keep our underarm above that imaginary line. The same is true for the forward swing. We can imagine, during our forward swing, that if we draw a line from our right underarm to the top of the ball, we could keep our right underarm above that imaginary line.

Try this to help you visualize the swing plane.

Hold your arms out in front of you on the swing plane, palms down. Visualize that your arms are long enough so that the palms of your hands can touch the top of the ball. Now, visualize a line from the top of the ball traveling along the bottom of your hands and arms to your underarms (at the shoulder connections) and continues on through your body. This is the swing plane. At the address position, let your hands hang naturally below the (white) swing plane line with the shaft of the club parallel to the line, as shown in Figure 42.

What the mind can't do is accurately visualize pointing to something we can't see behind our head.

I see so many people in a fixed backswing position with their heads turned, looking at their hands at the top of the backswing. They turn their heads, put their hands in some wonderful spot at the top of the backswing and stare at them. Then they swing with a completely different shoulder plane and their hands never reach that wonderful imaginary spot.

Our eyes cannot see behind, and it's very difficult for our computer (the brain) to imagine a position it cannot see. The natural shoulder and arm plane dictates the final position of the hands at the top of the backswing.

With the correct grip, lower body movement, and shoulder plane, your hands will set in a natural position at the top of the backswing.

As in Figure 45, when you have completed your backswing, you should be able to drop your hands a little and *the club shaft will hit the tip of your right shoulder.*

You can see the shoulder swing plane—as depicted by the dashed line in Figure 46—is *too flat*. The right underarm is below the swing plane set by the left shoulder. When you swing from this position, you feel like the club gets stuck behind you.

Fig. 45

Using your own natural aiming abilities will give you a more constant shoulder plane. Natural leg action along with a natural shoulder plane will set your hands in the proper position. Use the following shoulder swing planes by visually aiming your underarms during the swing:

1. Aiming (underarms) at the bottom of the ball (6 o'clock), **fade** (ball flight curves slightly left to right).

2. Aiming (underarms) lower than the bottom of the ball (6 o'clock) say between the ball and toes of your shoes, **slice** (ball flight curves sharply left to right).

3. Aiming (underarms) at the top of the ball (12 o'clock), **draw** (ball flight curves slightly right to left).

4. Aiming (underarms) higher than the top of the ball (12 o'clock), **hook** (ball flight curves sharply right to left).

Fig. 46

While practicing at the range, pretend there is a tree right in front of you about fifty to a hundred yards away. Pick out a target line to the right and align your stance with that target. Now flatten your shoulder swing by visually aiming your underarms at the top of the ball (12 o'clock). *The shots should go out and around the imaginary tree turning left or drawing.*

Now pick out a target to the left of your imaginary tree and align your stance with that target. Steeping your shoulder swings, aim your underarms at the bottom of the ball (6 o'clock). The shots should go out and around the imaginary tree, turning right or fading.

Align your setup a little right and aim your draw shot down the right side of the fairway, so the ball will finish in the middle of the fairway. It is vice versa for the fade.

Think of swinging an ax or sledge hammer with the hands gripping on the backside of the ax handle. The swing and grip are very similar to the golf swing. When swinging an ax at waist, knee or ankle high, your shoulders are basically flat, turning back and forth. You would not swing an ax dipping your left shoulder on the back swing and then dipping your right shoulder on the forward swing. Otherwise, you don't swing in a u-shaped motion, but turn your shoulders in a flatter motion, very similar to the golf swing.

Think of having a 4 foot by 8 foot piece of plywood, the 4 foot wide part sitting flat on top of the golf ball and the 8 foot flat length of plywood goes from the top of the golf ball, right through your body just below your arm pits. Now, when you swing, think of having your arm pits touching, at all times, the flat surface of the plywood throughout the swing. Never having your arm pits below the surface of the plywood (draw or hook) and below surface (fade or slice).

HOW FAST DO YOU SWING THE GOLF CLUB IN YOUR BACKSWING?

Only wind up your golf swing as fast as your shoulders move, not as fast as your arms move.

Allowing your shoulders to dictate your arm swing enhances swing timing. That's why we want to lift the left heel, in conjunction with starting the left shoulder and hip rotation. Your shoulder and body turn dictate your backswing speed. Prevent your arms from dictating the speed of the backswing. The same is true for the forward swing. Lift your right heel and rotate your right leg, hip and shoulder back to the left. Keep the arms from dictating the timing of the forward swing or starting your forward swing from the top. The top is where your hands stop in the backswing and start forward.

*Poor lower body and shoulder rotation allows
the arms to dictate the swing speed.*

You want to think that your back swing takes as long as it takes to say, slowly *one thousand and one,* as you start rotating forward on one. That's how long it takes to rotate the left shoulder in the backswing from address position to turning right and stopping just above the right foot. With arm swings only, it is likely you will not have time to say, (unless you say it really fast), *nine eighty-nine* as you start rotating forward on eighty-nine.

If the arm swing gets ahead of the shoulders, you will be in the ball striking area before your right heel clears the ground. This increases the chance to top the ball, hands in the swing being ahead of your lower body action.

You want to have your right side in motion with the heel off the ground, before your hands or club head reach the ball striking area.

Use the big muscles in your legs, back and shoulders for distance, not just the little muscles in your forearms and wrist. Put your shoulders and legs into your golf swing. Wait for your shoulders to completely turn to the maximum.

Use the drill we started earlier, with the club behind your back. This will teach you to use your upper and lower body properly for starting both the backswing and the forward swing.

THE RIGHT ELBOW WORKS AS A LEVER IN THE FORWARD SWING

Another distance robber is premature straightening or uncoiling of the right arm. This occurs when your lower body is not working. It forces you to arm swing from the top at the start of the forward swing.

A reverse weight shift, or swinging with the weight on your right foot, will encourage an arm swing and the premature uncoiling of your right elbow. *The right elbow is the lever needed for distance in the forward swing.*

Let's say you are a right-handed pitcher and you throw a fast ball towards home plate with a straight right arm. Without using your elbow as a lever, you will not have a fast ball. You cannot throw a fast ball with an extended straight arm. In order to throw a fast ball, you must have a lever (your elbow joint). The right shoulder and legs start the pitching motion. The elbow (lever) will be leading and coiled, closer to home plate, adjacent to the shoulder and ahead of the right hand with the ball, as shown in Figure 47.

The right hand and forearm pivot through when the elbow (lever) has reached its maximum pivotal point of release, as show in Figure 48.

In the golf forward swing, it's like throwing a fast ball, but on a different plane. We must have the elbow leading and coiled until we are into the ball striking area. One of the reasons you want to get off of your right side at the start of the forward swing is to prevent your right elbow from uncoiling prematurely. Weight remaining on your right leg, or reverse shifting of weight to your right leg, will cause your left shoulder to open to the left. This will cause your right arm to prematurely uncoil and eliminate the lever. The result is a loss of direction and distance. Keep the right elbow close to your side as long as possible, on the forward swing.

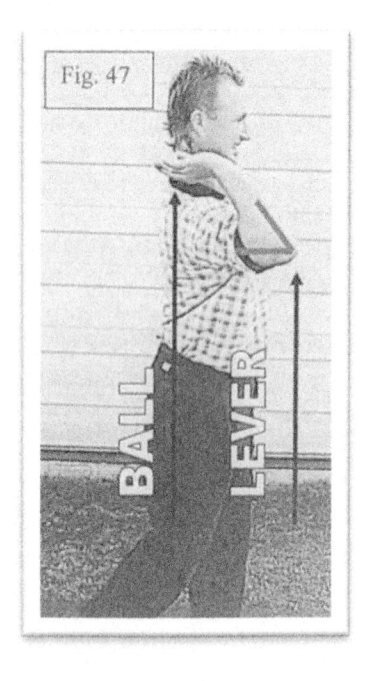

THE RIGHT ARM MOVEMENT IS LIKE SKIPPING ROCKS

This motion is like skipping rocks across the water. Try skipping a rock with a straight right arm and not using your body. *Nothing happens.* You must use the elbow as a lever. The elbow must be coiled or cocked like a lever and be leading or ahead of the rock, as shown in Figure 48.

If you try to skip rocks without your shoulder, hip and right knee rotating forward, your lever will uncoil and you will be forced to throw the rocks to the left of your target or across your body.

Without natural body movements, you cannot throw or hit your target with any regularity. If you try to hit golf balls without your right shoulder, hip and knee rotating, your lever will uncoil and you will hit the ball left of your target. This is because your body movements force you to swing across your body.

In terms of golf, try this: Address the ball with a golf club. Rotate your right elbow inward to the left until you visualize that the inside of your right arm at the elbow is lined up with the back of the ball. This is where the maximum pivotal point will occur during the uncoiling and pivoting through the right forearm and hands in the ball striking area. With the proper uncoiling of the body, and by using your large right shoulder muscles, your lever (elbow) will still be coiled when it arrives in the ball striking area. Then it's like a catapult launching the ball.

Your right elbow will be adjacent to your right hip during rotation. Be aware of your right shoulder plane while practicing or concentrating on your right elbow position.

While working on your right elbow in the swing, it is possible to create too steep a shoulder plane at the top of the backswing. That is where your right underarm drops below your imaginary plane. This can happen if you are trying to keep your elbow close to your side. It is also possible on the forward swing to create a steep right shoulder plane while trying to keep your elbow close to your hip in the ball striking area. This happens when you allow your right underarm swing to drop below your imaginary swing plane.

Keep your right underarm on plane above the ball, and the back of your left and right hand rotating towards the ball and the target line. Make as long a follow through as possible towards the target with your right shoulder.

Put your right elbow into your golf swing. At the top of the backswing, as you start forward, say to yourself, *throw the ball* or *skip the rock*. While practicing, remember to make three full swings without resetting the club behind the ball. The mind wants to take thumbnail pictures of the swing task we are working on. Too much analysis causes paralysis!

The mind and body will learn and comprehend swing tasks faster if we concentrate on the full swing and not just little parts of it.

GOLF IS A TWO-HANDED GAME

The right hand is providing most of the club head speed and power. The left hand provides some of the club head speed and power but mostly support, depth, lag and guidance in the impact area.

If you have the arm strength, you can practice swinging or hitting a golf ball one handed.

Here is how to swing one-handed:

First put your hands on the club in a normal grip. Keeping your right hand on the club in its normal position, remove your left hand and put it behind your back with your right hand in its normal position not at the end of the grip. Swing the club right hand only. Now take your normal grip with both hands and put your right hand behind your back and swing the club with your left hand only, placed at the end of the grip.

1. Place your right hand down from end of club grip in a normal hitting position. Take your full back swing, letting your right arm and elbow bend, as if holding a serving tray with your right hand at the top of the backswing, wrist cocked, palm flat, pointing skyward.

2. On the forward swing, try to imagine you are throwing a ball on the swing plane. Rotate or roll your wrist action through the hitting zone.

3. Say these two phrases to yourself *backswing* and *throw the ball*. Do this while initiating items one and two.

Use your footwork to rotate your body on the forward swing and keep your right arm from uncoiling until you reach the ball striking area, which is from right hip to the ball.

You can also swing your left arm alone.

Grip the club with your left hand in the normal position and put your right hand behind your back. While raising your left heel partially to facilitate the turn, swing the club to the right up into the backswing position, left arm straight, wrist cocked, hips turned slightly left. Pause. Drop left heel, start turning hips left, and sweep your left arm forward just like when holding the club with both hands. Your wrist unhinges and the club head touches the ground as the left hand rolls over and through the hitting zone. The follow through should happen naturally, as your arm moves right to left. Your arm and club head will point to the target, the left elbow bends because your left arm continues sweeping upward in the finish as your momentum and left shoulder pull the arm upward.

1. Keep your left arm as straight as possible on the backswing, lifting your left heel and turning your body will help keep it straight.

2. Cock your left wrist from waist high to the top of the backswing.

3. In the hitting area of the forward swing, from waist high to the ball, keep the left end or butt of the golf club

handle pointing at the ball and towards the target as long as you can. In an instant, your left hand will release and rotate with the back of your hand now facing the target on the forward swing, as the club head impacts with the ball.

4. The left arm folds at the elbow and finishes over your left shoulder with the wrist fully cocked—Figure 53.

5. At the finish of the follow-through, you should be able to open your left hand like you would be carrying a food serving tray.

Remember, use your footwork and rotate your body. It is important in this one-handed exercise to keep speeding up the unhinging and rolling your right and left hands through the impact zone, which is from right hip to the ball.

Finish this one-handed drill with both hands on the club, gripping in their normal position, while swinging.

Whenever you're working on any swing task, always reinsert that task back into the full swing. Do this by using the continuous three swings method (see Chapter One).

THE PROPER ADDRESS POSITION AND SWING MOTIONS

The address position is shown in Figure 49:

- Your right shoulder will be a little lower than your left.
- Your right hand is lower on the club.

Fig. 49

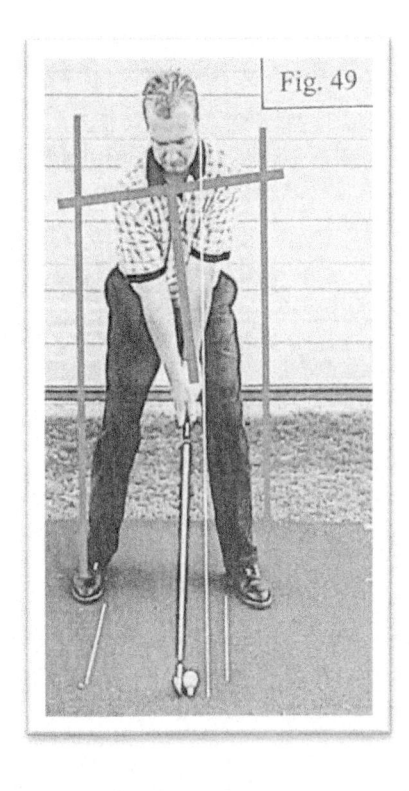

- Your head will be in back of the ball.
- Your upper body is tipped above the waist back towards your right foot slightly to line ball up on left cheek.
- Imagine the ball being even with or sitting on the left side of your face.
- The back of your upper left arm will rest on the chest pectoral muscles.
- Your stance width will be as wide as the inside of your insteps and the width of your shoulders.

The width of your stance should never be so wide that the weight is not directly over the right foot or slightly on the instep on the back swing. During the forward swing, the left side of your upper body will rotate under your left arm in the ball striking area—Figure 50.

Do not address the ball with level shoulders and your left arm against your side. If your upper left arm is at your side and your chest is big, the body, as it rotates back to the left, will push on your upper left arm in the ball striking area.

This will cause your left shoulder to move left of the target line before the right side of the body gets into the ball impact area. The club head will quickly move inside, resulting in a miss hit.

Try this at address.

As in Figure 51, place your right hand flat on your left pectoral chest muscle, with your fingers straight. Now raise your left arm, keeping it straight. Place the back of your left arm covering your fingers in the right hand. As shown in Figure 51, this position will allow the left side of the body to rotate under the left arm in the hitting area.

Fig. 50

This set up position will allow the left shoulder to remain pointing a little right of the target until the right side of the body gets into the club and ball impact area of the swing arc.

Look at the left hand in Figure 50. The left hand and forearms will roll towards the target *and the glove logo or back of your left hand will be pointing towards the target at impact.* Visualize at the beginning of the swing that the back of the left hand will return to the back of the ball facing the target.

Unless you are what I would call a right foot hitter, your weight remains on the right foot during the forward swing. Your left shoulder would be forced to turn left as far as your left hip. Your head would be up, following or being pulled along by your left shoulder. Your hands would be pulled away and over the left knee. You would be falling back from the ball at impact, and you will not be able to return the glove logo or back of the hand to the back of the ball pointing at the target.

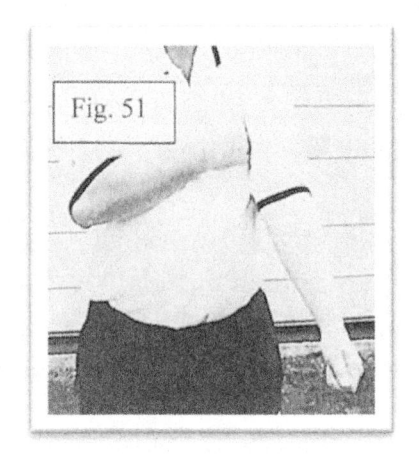

Fig. 51

Let's digress a little.

Golf is a two-handed game. The left hand takes on the role of supporting and guiding. You can hit a ball with just your left hand, but as with most right handers, the force in your swing comes from the right with the rotation of body, arms and release of the right elbow and forearm. The elbow is the lever. Some people think the power is in the left hand. I disagree with this train of thought. If I was a right-handed fast ball pitcher, I would not throw to the plate with my left arm backhanded. Similarly, if I were pounding a spike in a tree, I would not hold the sledgehammer in my left hand and pound backhanded. During the swing, the left arm is straight at impact with the ball. The force to the left hand comes from centrifugal force from the uncoiling of the body and its rotation on the forward swing. Keeping the butt of the club pointing at the ball on the forward swing as long as possible will help hold the right elbow against the right hip.

SWING MOMENTUM AND TOTAL EXTENSION OF THE ARMS PULLS THE HEAD UP

In Figure 52, we can see a portion of the desired follow-through. The arms have both rotated and reached total extension. From this point, your left elbow will fold and forward momentum will pull your head up into a completed follow-through.

- From impact with the ball and forward, your forearms will rotate to the left.
- Your body weight from the weight shift and momentum is on the forward outside edge of your left foot.
- Your right heel is swinging to a vertical point while pivoting on your right toe.
- Your head is being pulled up into a finish from your arms reaching full extension.
- Your head will be pulled up to a finished position and you are looking at the target.
- Your left shoulder has moved left over the left hip.

You can only reach this position by having your weight off your right foot. In Figure 53, we can see that forward from the point where the arms are fully extended, the left arm will collapse at the elbow and finish folded. At the completion of the follow through, your left hand will be supporting the club with your palm facing skyward. If you opened your left hand, you could support a serving tray.

Also, looking at Figure 53, we see the results of the full follow-through. *The hands and arms are away from the head.* The hands are over the tip of the left shoulder to counter balance the head being slightly tipped to the right.

Try tapping the tip of your left shoulder with the shaft. *Do not keep your forearms and wrist stiff when completing the follow through. Let the arms bend and the hands return to a full cocked position.* The right toe is a balancing point. The right knee is flexed and has moved over towards the left knee. The left leg is supporting the body with the knee joint straight and locked in position.

Fig. 53

If due to operations and bone ailments you can't, just using some of the aforementioned body and foot motions with the heels will help you greatly in getting your flexibility back.

You, too, can finish in this position.

Try this *without a golf club.*

Place your arms at your side. Turn to the left with the toe of your right foot as a pivot point and face the target, as in a full follow through. Let your upper body tip slightly to the right. Now, while standing with most of your weight on your left foot in balance, reach and place your hands over your left shoulder in a fully cocked position. Keep your hands and arms relaxed and as far away from the head as possible. Finish the swing with your head up, tipped slightly to the right looking past your arms, hands by your left shoulder while watching your ball going down the fairway or towards your target.

While practicing at the driving range, try to finish in this position. This is especially true when you are taking three continuous swings without stopping to reset the club behind the ball after each swing.

THE TAKEAWAY OR START OF THE BACKSWING

The start of the backswing is known as the takeaway. It begins as a *one-piece movement*. To practice, take a golf club and stand up straight, facing forward. Make sure the back of your left arm is resting on your pectoral muscle. *Without turning your left shoulder,* move your left arm cross your body until your left elbow wants to bend, as shown in Figure 54. This is as far as the left arm moves on its own during the backswing. The rest of the left arm movement is accomplished using the lower body and shoulder rotation.

Start the backswing with a simultaneous body rotation that uses your left heel, hips, shoulders, and arms.

The start of the backswing should be unhurried, letting the big muscles in the legs and shoulders dictate the swing speed.

We do not hit anything on our backswing, so there is no need for excess speed. The club is going to come to a stop anyway when it reverses directions.

Try saying to yourself while taking the backswing, *one—thousand—and—one*. Start the forward swing upon completion of the words *and one*.

The shoulder rotation will help in the movement of your arms. So, let your shoulder rotation and swing plane dictate the arm position and speed throughout the backswing.

Fig. 54

SWINGING IN A CIRCLE

Imagine a large wagon wheel lying flat on the ground, and you are standing, at address, on the hub of the wagon wheel. At address, the clubface will face the target with the club head resting on the side of the wagon wheel. Your clubface will be 90 degrees (right angle) to the wagon wheel or circle. The clubface remains 90 degrees to the circle throughout the whole swing.

For example, take a partial backswing, rotating your arms to the right as you swing back to where your arms are waist high and the toe of club head is pointing skyward. Hold that position. Now lower your arms and place the club head down on the wheel. At this point in the backswing, your clubface will still be 90 degrees to the circle and lined up with the wagon wheel spoke. It is facing the same way as the green arrow dash line in the wagon wheel drawing. Imagine setting the club head down on the wheel at every one of the wooden spokes during the backswing, from the start to waist high. *The clubface will always be 90 degrees (right angle) to the circle.* Consequently, the same is true for the forward swing. The face of the club will always be in line with the wooden spokes or right angle to the circle. At waist high of the follow-through, the toe of the club will be pointing skyward. It is a mirror image to the backswing.

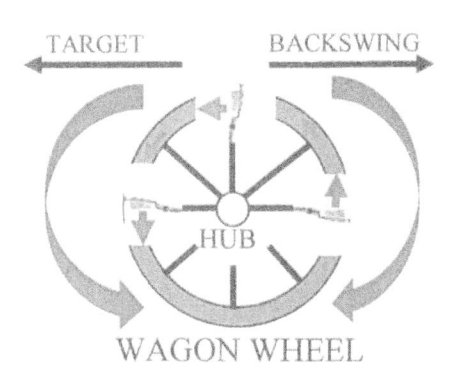

See the green arrows in the wagon wheel detail.
Each one represents the direction the clubface would be facing.

You *do not* want to make the start of your backswing using a quick movement with your hands and wrist. The body rotation will lag too far behind. Your club will be coming to the inside too quickly. When this happens, the club will not remain

90 degrees to the circle. This movement causes your hands and arms to reroute at the top of the backswing, in order to move into the proper forward swing. The result is inconsistency in ball striking and ball direction.

Also, *do not* take your backswing with the clubface continuously pointing at the target. This will restrict the natural arm rotation and the club will not remain 90 degrees to the circle. This movement causes the arms and hands to reroute at the top of the backswing, in order to move into the forward swing. Again, the result is inconsistency in ball striking and ball direction.

The natural rotation of the arms during the backswing and forward swing will keep the clubface at a right angle to the circle. Any disruption of this natural rotation will not let the clubface stay at 90 degrees.

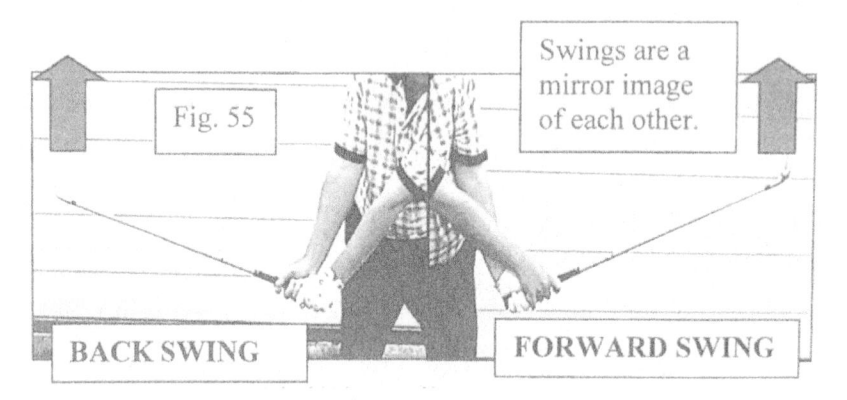

Fig. 55

Swings are a mirror image of each other.

BACK SWING　　FORWARD SWING

In Figure 55, we can see the backswing with the rotation of the body and shoulders. The club has rotated with a natural arm rotation and the toe of the club head is pointing skyward at waist high. The forward swing is a mirror image when a natural arm rotation happens. Again, with the rotation of the body and shoulders, the arms come to full extension with the toe of the club head pointing skyward.

Try practicing a partial swing. Swing the club to waist high in both directions without stopping to reset the club. Use your feet, lift your heels, and remember your body and shoulder rotations as in a full swing. Have the toe of the club point skyward both on your backswing and forward swing.

HANGING ON TOO LONG WITH THE LEFT HAND

You hear this on the range and golf course, too. What is happening when someone says you're hanging on too long with the left hand?

Three things are happening.

1. The right shoulder plane is too steep and you physically can't release the club through the ball striking area.

2. A steep right shoulder swing forces your left hip quickly to the left, causing a blocking action or resistance to swing at the target. This is because the arms and hands are trying to follow the hips to the left.

3. A steep shoulder swing plane forces your hips too quickly to the left. This forces the left hand to be too far out in front and you are not able to release the hands

properly. After you have swung, you feel that the left hand was forced to over grip or do all the work.

Two things need to be done to eliminate these problems.

1. Flatten your right shoulder swing plane on your forward swing while keeping your right elbow close to your side with right underarm aimed above the ball.

2. Get off your right side quicker, using your right heel and making sure your body is rotating.

Both will keep your left and right shoulder and hip actions intact and allow the proper release of your hand action.

COMING OVER THE TOP AND TOO MUCH RIGHT HAND

You hear this on the range and golf course, too. What you see is a pulled and uncontrollable hook going sharply left. What is really happening? Usually, your right shoulder plane is above the ball, and if everything else were in position, you would be hitting the ball down the right side of the fairway with a nice five to ten-foot draw. The problems that cause these two swing errors are similar.

Three things are actually happening.

1. You are aligned too far to the right. This alignment is blocking your left hip on the forward swing. This does not allow the hip to rotate to the left.

2. Your alignment is forcing your arms to initiate the start of the forward swing and they come out of the swing plane at the beginning of the forward swing.

3. Your left shoulder plane is too steep on the backswing. This forces the weight to remain on the left side during the backswing. The weight then reverses back to the right side on the forward swing. It forces the left shoulder left or to spinout.

The results of this incorrect swing are that the ball flight starts left of your target. If you add the five to ten-foot draw, it looks like a big hook. In reality, the ball was heading left from the start. The feelings are that you struck the ball completely with your right hand and swung over the top on your forward swing.

Five things need to be done to eliminate these problems.

1. Correct your alignment, back foot 90 degrees to target line, like railroad tracks and forward foot slightly flared out.

2. Flatten out your left shoulder plane, underarm aimed above the ball.

3. Start your lower body on the right side sooner during the forward swing. Use your heels.

4. Make sure on the follow-through that your right shoulder follows down the target line as long as possible.

5. Keep the butt of the club pointing at the ball longer on your forward swing with your elbow on your right hip. Feel like you are hitting the ball in the center of your right hand and at impact the palm is pointing at the target while it rolls through.

TOO MUCH HOOK

This happens if you get too flat with your shoulder swing plane and don't follow through enough with your right shoulder. Get a feeling of swinging past impact with your forearms towards the target. If you don't, the result is a big hook. The difference is the ball will start out to the right and then curve too sharply to the left.

To eliminate this, steepen your shoulder swing plane slightly, follow through completely with your right shoulder and forearms until you get a nice draw and not the uncontrolled hook.

TOO MUCH SLICE

Here you get too steep with the shoulder swing planes. Your alignment and shoulder planes are too steep. You are forcing the club head left across the face of the ball.

To correct this:

1. Flatten out your shoulder plane, get the weight off your back foot.

2. Improve your leg action so the right hip area and lower body are starting the forward swing. Use your heels.

3. Check your alignment and back foot that it is not flared out to the right but perpendicular (90 degrees) to the target line. This can be a very big fault in the golfer's alignment, causing tension in the lower body on the forward swing along with slicing or pushing the ball to the right. Basically, preventing 1 and 2 above.

CHAPTER FIVE
Equipment

Having the right equipment can make a difference. This means having equipment that fits your body, posture, and your swing speed.

Not all golfers are the same height. Nor do they generate the same swing speed. Not all golfers have the same arm and leg lengths.

If your golf equipment does not fit your swing in each one of these areas, it will affect ball flight and distance.

That's why golf equipment manufacturers make a myriad of golf equipment changes for the same style of clubs. You can buy shafts for your clubs that fit different swing speeds, and have different shaft stiffness, flex points, weight, and length. Also, you can purchase a selection of different shaft materials such as steel and graphite.

Picking the right shaft for your game is the most important thing when choosing equipment.

The wrong golf club shaft can affect the ball flight, even if you swing perfectly. Too stiff a shaft will cause you to lose distance and prevent you from getting the ball airborne easily. Too flexible a shaft will cause inconsistent shots. Faded and sliced golf shots often happen because the clubhead is lagging behind and open at impact. Or snap hooks occur because the club head passes the hands in a shut position.

Here is how to pick the right club shaft for your swing.

If you have hit many balls at a range or golf shop, you are swinging about ten percent faster than you would on a golf course. The reason is that on the golf course you have a lot more time between shots. On a golf range, you are hitting one ball after the other. Your muscles are looser and creating a faster swing speed.

Let's say the swing speed instrument at the range or golf shop shows your swing speed at 90 mph. Ten percent of 90 mph is 9 mph. On the golf course your swing speed will drop down to 81 mph. You would want to buy a set of clubs with a swing speed between 80 and 90 mph not between 70 and 80 mph nor 90 and 100 mph.

The second most important thing is the lie angle of the head of the golf club.

The head of the golf club lie angle should fit your body posture. For instance, imagine you are six feet tall with long arms. With a standard set of clubs, your swing might be digging the heel of the club into the ground. You should be swinging clubs with a plus lie angle. If you are six-feet tall with short arms, you might be digging the toe of the club into the ground. You should be swinging clubs with a minus lie angle.

Before making a major purchase, check with your local driving range or golf shop equipment professional.

An equipment professional can measure your lie angle on a swing board along with your swing speed. The equipment professional will put a piece of tape on the bottom of your club or a test club. After you swing, the Pro can look at the tape and see if the scratch marks are in the center, which is just right. If the scratch marks are on the heel, you need a plus lie angle. If the scratch marks are on the toe, you need a minus lie angle. The club fitting professional can bend the club slightly, so the mark on the tape on the bottom flange of the club head is right in the middle.

Also, the grip of the club can be made larger to fit larger hands or longer fingers. Most right-handed golfers wear a golf glove on their left hand for a better grip.

Golf balls vary.

There are wound golf balls, two and three-piece balls, surlyn covered, elastomeric covered, and different compression consistencies and number of dimples. Try different golf balls to find one that feels good to you and one you have confidence in controlling. Find a ball that fits your total game, not just your driving distance alone.

Most golf shops have a swing station to hit balls indoors. The swing station is set up so you see on a screen your ball flight, distance, spin rotation and other important statistics. This information is free, and you will be able to try all brands of clubs and find just the right one for you. Remember, if it feels a little harsh or stiff there, it will feel harsher and stiffer on the golf course with more time between shots and a slightly slower swing speed.

CHAPTER SIX
Practice and Playing Procedures

Excluding the extra-long putters, the driver is the longest club in the golf bag. Let's say you hit ten balls at a target with a seven iron and then with the longest club, the driver. Due to an error in your swing, the average distance from the target left or right is ten yards with the seven iron. Due to the difference in club length between the driver and the seven iron, the error in your swing is compounded, and the ball slices right or hooks left twenty-five-yards away from your intended target.

> *If there is an error in your swing, it will be magnified by each inch of difference in length between the two clubs.*

Too many people see this large disparity in accuracy and try to improve their swing by practicing with a driver. Try hitting ten balls with a driver, just as hard as you can possibly swing. Then after a few minutes of rest, try hitting five balls at a smooth relaxed tempo. Which balls could you find on the golf course? After you have hit ten balls in a row with a driver, your muscles start stretching. The first few balls you hit go pretty well. Then you hit one to the right and you adjust. You hit one to the left and you make another adjustment. Soon you are all over the range with your accuracy. You get another bucket of balls and hit them with a driver. You leave the range not in a positive state of mind but in *complete disgust.* Practicing should be just the opposite.

Always leave the range with a positive mind set. The swing you are learning is for both metal woods and irons. There is not a special swing for each club. You have one basic swing for all clubs, but you can subtly change the swing—as mentioned earlier—for special shots, hitting higher or lower, or a little left or right.

When learning the golf swing, I suggest you stay with the *eight, seven, and six irons.* These clubs will help you stay in a positive mind set. With these clubs, you can feel what is going on in your swing. When you get proficient with these clubs, move up to a five iron. If you have trouble, go back to the six or seven iron. Keep trying to move up the irons to the woods. If you have trouble, back down on the irons until you start hitting proficiently again.

Fig. 56

Remember, the longer the club shaft the more the swing error is magnified.

As shown in Figure 56, you can set up a swinging station by laying two clubs down to help your alignment. Place one club by your hitting area, pointing at your target. Place the other near your toe line parallel to the club facing your target.

Some like to lay a third club in alignment with the golf ball one or two inches inside the left heel.

This is one way the professional golfers warm up prior to the beginning of a tournament. They hit a few wedges or nine irons to loosen their muscles. They hit a lot of eight, seven, and six irons for accuracy and make minor swing adjustments. They might hit a couple of punch shots or draw and fade shots. They hit a few fairway wood shots or long irons and maybe five or six drives. You will not see them hit hundreds with their driver. They want to leave the range with a very positive mind set. Some will come back and finish with a favorite wedge to relax and then set off to the putting green.

THE SUBCONSCIOUS AND THE SHORT GAME

How to diminish three putting and get rid of the three-foot yip.

I am going to help you with a few basics around the putting green. I also will suggest two easy putting drills to improve your short game. Both of these practice exercises will force your subconscious to do the work.

Once you trust your subconscious, you're on your way.
Let your subconscious putt, not you!

Let's say you are a second baseman throwing the baseball to first base. You look over at first base. Your eyes feed you the distance, and not only tell your muscles how hard to throw, but in what direction. Now imagine, you had to throw to first base but with a sack over your head so you couldn't see. You could still make the throw to first base, letting your subconscious take over. If someone is standing just three feet from you, you wouldn't rare back and throw the ball real hard. Your subconscious estimates what is needed based on the visual pictures in your mind.

In the morning when we shave, we don't pick up the shaving cream and say this is the best shave I am ever going to give myself. You don't tell yourself: put the shaving cream in my left hand, put my right hand in the shaving cream, put the shaving cream on my face, now pull down on the razor. No, you shave thinking about dropping off the kids or paying bills or meeting someone. When you finish you look fine?

Obviously, your subconscious is going to do a better job. Your subconscious has been trained over the years without you paying too much attention on giving yourself a good shave.

Your subconscious will work for you the same way on the putting green. On the practice putting green, pace off about seven full strides or say, twenty-one feet. At this distance, you will not be able to see the hole with your peripheral vision. You will be like the second baseman with the sack over his head. Pick out a relatively flat putt. Put two coins on the green about eighteen inches apart and place them perpendicular to your putting line. Place four balls between the coins. Prepare to putt all four balls. Take a few practice putts looking at the hole before you hit the first putt.

Now I want you to putt all four balls at the hole without looking where they go. Try to visualize where the hole is. Remember, absolutely no peeking! After you have putted your last ball, look up and take several moments to let your subconscious take into account where the balls have finished.

They may be all short of the hole; they may be all five feet past, or all left, or all right. Let your subconscious see how they have finished. Then do this over again. You will start making minor adjustments. Think of each ball going in the hole.

After repeating this putting practice about twelve times, you will hear the balls going into the hole.

Not looking where each ball will finish forces your subconscious to do the work. Putting two balls and always looking where each ball will finish, forces the subconscious to go on vacation.

Now putt all four balls by lining up your putter behind the ball and staring at the hole. Do not look down at the ball after your putter is lined up.

While staring at the hole, the only thing you should be thinking about is, "I want to putt the ball this hard to sink the putt." Then putt the ball. Do this exercise about twelve times?

Next, reduce your length to six feet. Put the coins out with four balls between them. Putt all four balls without looking at least twelve times. I know that at six feet you can see the hole out of the corner of your eye.

Now putt all four balls while looking at the hole only and think, "I need to stroke the ball this hard to hole it." The last thing you do while putting is take one last look at the hole thinking, "I want to putt the ball this hard to hole it."

Whether twenty-one feet or six feet from the hole, if you putt looking only at the hole and are certain to make good contact with the putter, you will putt better. You will constantly get information for your muscles from the eyes. When putting, you are looking down at the putter head and ball, not at your target. It's like someone put a sack over your head; you can't see the hole. You must trust your subconscious to know how hard to strike the ball and on what line.

If you putt two balls on the putting green for ten minutes looking at each putt, you're not forcing your subconscious to do the work. The mind can be trained to read twenty thousand words a minute. How dull or boring it must be for the mind to concentrate on one little thing in this big green area!

At the moment of impact, where the putter strikes the ball, you can only think of one thing at a time. That will be either the putting line or how hard to hit the putt. If you think about line, your subconscious doesn't know how hard to hit the ball, and you usually come up short.

So, pick your line first and then concentrate on how hard to strike the ball.

Take a practice swing on long putts and visualize the ball rolling the total distance. If you have a fifty-foot putt, pick out the line first, and then practice swing and visualize how long it would take to get there. Now practice swing thinking, *I will hit the ball this hard to roll it to the hole.*

You can also use these exercises around the green while chipping. Try chipping five balls about ten paces or thirty feet without looking at the hole. Take your putter and try to one putt each of five balls. Each ball is worth twenty percent. Try to get to a hundred percent. You can use this exercise with different clubs.

Now, I want you to try putting from off the green, but first, let's discuss the practice method.

Many golfers putting from off the green try to control the physical and mental part of the putt.

Golfers don't trust their subconscious. Think of it this way: If the green side putt were on a piece of glass tipped towards the hole, your mind's eye would see this and relate the information to the subconscious. We would let the subconscious putt for us and barely tap the putt. Also, if the grass were wet and a little longer, your mind's eye would see this and relate the information to your subconscious. If the grass were three feet tall, you surely would know to swing the putter harder. Here's the method to use for putting from off the green. Pick out the line, take a practice stroke or two, and think, *"I want to hit the ball this hard to roll it six inches past the hole."* Then let your subconscious putt. *Don't try to help.*

BEING IN THE ZONE

We have learned that your subconscious plays a big role in the short game. How about the long game? If you had a shot from one hundred and fifty yards, you would do better if you had special eyesight. This special eyesight would allow you to look at the flag and the ball simultaneously, while swinging. You would have constant input from your special eyes telling your muscles how hard to swing and in what direction. You would be looking at both the target and the ball.

But in reality, after we look at the target, we turn away and look at the ball three feet in front of us. This is like putting a sack over our head; we think we have the direction, but we can no longer see the target. If you have practiced a lot or played a lot, you will have the subconscious to help you relax and leave the swinging of the club to your subconscious. If you are just beginning, you can see how practice can help train your subconscious for the tasks ahead. Like eating lemon meringue pie, your subconscious remembers how it tastes. Good golfers look at a golf shot and feel how they accomplished it before. They address the ball and in the instant before swinging, the subconscious takes over and the swing starts. Some days you are in the zone. Like looking in the mirror after shaving, it looks good but you can't remember the shaving details.

NERVES, PRESSURE AND FEAR

Often at the first tee, you're unsure of yourself. You are a good golfer and you know that everybody is watching. Or, you are in a golf match and you think your opponent is better. All these things cause you to be nervous.

It is very hard to calm yourself down when your heart is pounding and you can hardly breathe.

Try to take a deep breath every few minutes and hold it until you can count to ten. Then let it out slowly.

By the time you reach the first tee you can calm your heart rate down. Sometimes it helps if you realize that you're not the only one who is nervous. You can imagine that everyone is nervous. Imagine they are so nervous that you can see their legs shaking and their knees rattling!

Try not to put undue pressure on yourself. Many golf rounds go badly because of undue pressure. If a person pars the last two holes in his golf round, it would be one of his best rounds ever. Now for the last two holes, he was trying to shoot his best golf round ever. This added too much pressure to the game. It ruined a good round of golf by going double bogey, triple bogey. Try to avoid things in your golf round that will put pressure on your game. Making large bets adds pressure. Thinking too much about your score adds pressure. Trying to make the impossible shot adds fear. None of these things help your golf game. Slow your heart rate down and take some deep breaths, letting your breath out slowly, counting slowly to eight or ten, whatever works for you.

SOME PLAYING PROCEDURES AND GOLF ETIQUETTE

Playing through the green. This terminology is from the Rules of Golf and changed in 2019 to refer to the general area of the course from tee box to the putting green.

- Who goes first is decided on the tee of the first hole.
- After leaving the tee box, the person farthest from the hole (flag) plays first. I will mention Ready Golf below, which means the person who is ready can hit, if the person farthest from the hole is not ready.
- Play continues until everyone is on the green (putting surface).
- Once all the balls are on the green, each player places a ball marker (often a small coin) behind their ball. Place your marker using the line from the hole to the ball as a reference point. After the ball is marked, you can pick it up. You may mark your ball off to one side, if your

marker is in the line of another player. Most golfers measure to one side using the length of the putter head.
- Only one person putts at a time and that is the player farthest from the hole.
- Each person will continue to putt the ball until it is holed out. See exception below.
- All players proceed to the next hole where the score will be tallied and the playing procedure is repeated with the lowest scorer going first. When finished putting, do not write down your score at the green, because it holds up the golfers behind you, who are trying to get on that green. If the low score is tied, then the person with the low score that went first off on the last hole goes first on this hole and the person who tied goes second (unless playing Ready Golf, then the person who is ready, hits the ball).

Etiquette in the tee area.
- Only one player tees off at a time.
- All other players stand off to one side. If you have to stand somewhere behind the player, try to stand as much as possible to one side. Try not to stand directly behind the player or in their line of play, because this is distracting and causes the person hitting the ball to think about you standing there instead of what they are doing.
- Always leave plenty of room for the player to swing.
- Always hold very still while someone else is playing and be very quiet.

- Always repair any damage like a divot in the grass caused by your club.

Etiquette through the green.
- Only one player plays his ball at a time.
- Hold very still and keep golf carts from moving while a person is preparing to swing or is actually swinging.
- Try not to stand or park your golf cart directly behind the player in his line of play.
- If for some reason you are out in front of a player preparing to play, make sure they are aware that you can see them and that you are watching while they are hitting.
- Rake your footprints while in a bunker, and again repair any damage such as divots in the grass caused by your club while striking the ball.
- Never hit the ball until the group in front of you is clear. If there is a chance that your ball may go that far, don't hit. Golfers do not like to hear golf balls bouncing up behind them. It makes them nervous.
- Power golf carts and handcarts should be placed in the area where the cart will be easily accessible leaving the green to proceed to the next hole. Players behind you should not have to wait while you retrieve the cart or golf bag before moving on.

Etiquette on the green.
- The player's line is the intended line the ball will roll on from point of origin to the hole.
- Be sure not to walk or step on any player's line.

Footprints and spike marks have been known to knock the golf ball off line while rolling through someone's footprint.
- Repair any divot on the green made by your golf ball while landing.
- The person furthest from the hole is first to play. That person may continue to play until the ball is holed out. That person may also discontinue putting and mark the ball, because they think they will be stepping on someone else's line. Then, the next farthest player will commence to play.
- Be very quiet and hold still while someone else is putting their ball.
- Stay out of a player's line of sight from behind where the ball lies to the hole and beyond the other side of the hole.
- Replace the flag before leaving the green. But recent rule changes allow the flag to stay in the hole, although a player may elect to take it out or leave it in.

READY GOLF

Increase your speed of play.
If you are not playing under tournament conditions, here are some suggestions to speed up your play. This is good when your group is falling behind, or if you are not able to keep up with the group in front of you.
- If you have two power golf carts, let the group in the first cart tee off first. They can be ready to pull out immediately upon completion of the second cart of

players hitting their golf balls. If you are in the second cart, do not put your clubs back in the bag. Instead, get in the cart, keeping your club, and head cover in your hand while traveling. Return your club to the golf bag when you arrive at your ball unless you need to use it again. Then it's already in your hand.
- If you are close to the next teeing area, the first two people finished putting should go to the next tee and tee off.
- Even though you're not further away, look at your putt while other players are looking at theirs. Be sure to not get in their way.
- Lost ball—your ball. In the past, you could spend five minutes looking for your ball. But since 2019, according to the Rules of Golf, you have three minutes to find it. Then it is deemed lost and you need to immediately hit another.
- Lost ball—someone else. Play your ball, if possible, then help other players look for their lost balls. But remember the three-minute rule.
- If you are a beginner, pick up your ball if you have already achieved triple bogey for the hole you are playing. But if no golfers are behind you, continue to play.
- If power carts are not allowed on the fairways and you have to leave your cart on the path and walk to your ball (common on some Par 3 holes), take at least three clubs with you, so you do not have to go back and forth to the cart to get the club you need.
- If there is any doubt that you might not find your ball

or that it might be out of bounds or in a hazard, hit a provisional ball before leaving the tee.
- If you are riding in a cart and come up to the green, and your ball is off the green and your partner is on, then grab your pitching wedge *and putter,* so you don't have to go back to the cart.
- Get the scores from the other players on the next tee. Don't sit next to the green and tally scores, because the players behind you are waiting to hit. This is especially important on Par 3 holes.

You notice I am not suggesting that you swing faster or putt quicker. If you do these little things, you will have plenty of time to play your ball.

The pressure from a group behind has ruined many golf rounds. If you are out of touch with the group in front of you, the best thing to do is let the faster group behind you play through. If you are in touch with the group in front, tell the group wanting to play through—in a pleasing way—there is no place for them to go. Mention that you are in touch with the group in front of you, and often waiting on them to hit. Let the Course Ambassador or Marshal settle any disputes. If the group behind you sees you doing the aforementioned things to speed up play, they tend to be more patient.

The golfers following you, will become very upset and impatient, if they see you doing the following:
- Moving like slow thick molasses.
- Calculating scores on the green before leaving.
- Walking very slowly.

- Taking twenty practice swings.
- Taking ten minutes to look at a putt.
- Taking a long time to put the clubs back in the golf bag.
- Slowly getting into the cart.

These golfers will tend to be *much less patient!*

For those in too much of a hurry I would say, if you don't have enough time to play a four hour or more round of golf, then don't go out. It's not worth ruining a round of golf for you, your friends, or the people in front of you because you have to catch a plane. Take time to relax. There's enough road rage to go around while driving without bringing it to the golf course. When you're a hundred years old, you won't remember the hour and a half you lost on the golf course when you were younger. I know when I am one hundred years old; I am not going to remember the time I lost. But I will remember to thank the Creator if I am still on the topside of the fairway grass and not underneath it.

PARTING SHOTS

I wish you the best in your golfing endeavors. Even if you have been handicapped with health or physical problems, you can use the instructions in this book to improve your golfing experience. Don't be afraid to improve or get out of your comfort zone. You now have the knowledge to go forward. It's never too late. Don't be the one to get the trophy in the next tournament for the highest score. You can be the one who walks down the fairway and talks to his friends. Don't be the one who is so far out in the boonies that they send a search party to find you. You can be the one who pays green fees for use of the fairways and greens, and not the one who is looking to see if the golf course has a reduced rate for out in the boonies or rough fees in lieu of green fees.

CONTACT INFORMATION

Need help?

If you have any questions or comments, please feel free to email me at **golfdale1@yahoo.com**.

GLOSSARY

Address
   The position you take while standing and facing the golf ball. Also known as the ball striking position, the golf stance, and the hitting position.

Backswing
   Swinging back to your right, starting with the club right behind the ball and continuing to the top of your backswing. The top of the backswing is where the swing motion pauses before starting the forward swing.

Birdie
   One stroke under the golf holes rated stroke difficulty or one under par for that golf hole.

Bogey
   One stroke over the golf holes rated stroke difficulty or one over par for that golf hole. For example, a four would be bogey on a Par 3 hole—one over par. A six would be double bogey on a Par 4 hole—two over par. An eight would be a triple bogey on a Par 5 hole—three over par. An eight would be a quadruple bogey on a Par 4 hole—four over par. (If you're not in a tournament, pick up your ball after reaching triple par/triple bogey.)

Draw
   The golf ball flight curves slightly from right to left.

Fade
   The golf ball flight curves slightly from left to right.

Forward Swing
   Upon completion of the backswing, the forward swing starts forward to the left towards the ball. The swing continues to its completion or follow-through. Some use the word downswing instead of forward swing. I teach that the backswing is not an upswing and the forward swing is not a downswing. I want you to always think of swinging through the ball on the forward swing not down at the ball on the downswing.

Grip (Club)
   The rubber covering or leather wrap on the handle of the golf club.

Hook
   The golf ball flight curves sharply from right to left.

Housel (Club)
   Where the club shaft enters the club head.

Golf Green
   The golf green is where you putt the ball with the putter into the hole. The practice putting green is designated for practicing putting.

Lie Angle

A term used by club manufactures and professional club fitters to personally fit clubs to your specifications. The hosel of the club head can be bent at different angles to coincide with the length of the arms and the distance the hands are from the ground. A tall person with short arms may require a plus lie angle (more upright angled shaft), while a short person with long arms may require a minus lie angle (a flatter angled shaft).

Par

In golf, each hole is rated for its stroke difficulty and distance. For instance, a Par 3 is rated at three strokes.

Shaft (Club)

Part of the golf club that the club head and club grip are attached to.

Slice

The golf ball flight curves sharply from left to right.

Shank

Hitting the ball straight right of the intended line of flight.

Takeaway

The initial start of the backswing.

Tee Area

A place designated on each hole to start play. Tee up means place the ball on a tee. The golf ball is placed on a golf tee in the tee area. Tee up between the designated tee markers. Tee off means to hit the ball.

Through The Green

All the area on the golf course from the tee box to the green.

Waggling

The continuous movement of the hands and club head at the address position, which can relax the hands and forearms before striking the ball.

AFTERWORD

If you enjoyed my golf instruction book, please give it a positive review on Amazon, or wherever you purchase your books, and tell your friends about it. I so want to teach the world to golf. Maybe you know a golfer grandchild, lady friend, or golfer buddy who might enjoy this book as a birthday or Christmas present. Feel free to study and master the techniques listed here then help others who are struggling with their game.

Remember, as in life, stay curious and keep practicing and learning, and golf will help you stay young.